The Therapeutic Use of Survivor-Offender Communication:

Three Sexual Abuse Intervention Models

Edited by James M. Yokley

Chapters by
Walter Bera, Jan Hindman, Lucy Hutchens,
Denise McGuire & James Yokley

Social Solutions Press, LLC
P.O. Box 444
North Myrtle Beach, SC

International Standard Book Number: 978-0-9832449-3-6
Library of Congress Control Number: 2018907090

First published in 1990 by The Safer Society Press, Box 24-B Orwell, VT under the title-
The Use of Victim-Offender Communication in the Treatment of Sexual Abuse:
Three Intervention Models, 110 pages.

Reprint edition 2018 by Social Solutions Press, LLC, P.O. Box 444, North Myrtle Beach, S.C. Published after update editing with permission from the assigned copyright representative under the title-
The Therapeutic Use of Survivor-Offender Communication:
Three Sexual Abuse Intervention Models, 113 pages.

ACKNOWLEDGMENTS

The editor would like to extend a very special thanks to Fay Honey Knopp of the Safer Society Press for her encouragement and support of his attempt to integrate the work of several treatment programs in the area of survivor-offender communication into a book on this controversial topic. Her trust and patience were much appreciated. The editor would also like to thank Sally Maxton of the Ohio Youth Services Network for providing an ongoing series of comprehensive youth sex offender seminars. These seminars continue to develop the specialty training and motivation necessary for those of us who are attempting to contribute to this treatment area.

CONTENTS

PREFACE

This monograph focuses on an emerging approach to the treatment of sexual abuse, the use of various forms of survivor-offender communication to promote the progress of both the survivor and offender through recovery/rehabilitation. The intervention models described in this book are currently conducted within the framework of three outpatient sex-offender treatment programs. All three intervention models are consistent with the primary principles of trauma-informed care involving: safety; trustworthiness/transparency; choice; collaboration and; empowerment.

Chapter 1 reviews the survivor-offender communication interventions currently employed in a number of outpatient settings along with the theoretical benefits and published results of these interventions. This chapter also lists the basic guidelines under which these interventions are conducted.

Chapter 2 describes a treatment program based on a Restitution Model. This approach emphasizes close coordination with the criminal justice system, adjunct paraprofessional staff, and a unique treatment scrapbook created by the offender, used to help the survivor work through present and future problems when they occur.

Chapter 3 describes a treatment program focusing on understanding interpersonal violence within a Systemic/Attributional Model. This model has the unique perspective of recognizing the larger social context of the abuse.

Chapter 4 describes a treatment component based on a Clinical Evaluation Model emphasizing cognitive-behavioral survivor-offender communication interventions. This component can be integrated into existing treatment programs and involves the unique approach of using psychological testing to evaluate survivor-offender interactions.

While each treatment model has its own philosophy, their intervention methods share a number of common features including:
1. The use of survivor-offender apology or clarification sessions along with other methods to foster a clear understanding in both the offender and survivor that the *offender* is fully responsible for initiating and maintaining the abusive relation- ship;
2. A focus on the safety of the survivor that includes careful observation and monitoring;
3. Methods of addressing the offender's cognitive distortions and developing under- standing/empathy for survivors.

This book provides clinicians with a series of survivor-offender communications that can be integrated into current treatment practices for the benefit of the survivors and offenders under their care who choose to participate. The authors are clinicians whose interventions were based on their clinical experience and training. Case examples are provided to illustrate the intervention techniques described in each treatment model.

CONTRIBUTORS

WALTER H. BERA, M.A., a Psychologist and Family Therapist, has extensive experience in the field of sexual abuse assessment, treatment, and prevention, including five years as a therapist in the PHASE Program, one of the largest outpatient adolescent sex- offender programs in the Midwest. His Masters degree research on a typology of adolescent sex offenders led to the development (with Michael O'Brien, M.A.) of a classification system used widely throughout the United States. He is currently completing his Ph.D. in Family Social Science at the University of Minnesota, maintaining a private practice, consulting/ speaking on sexual abuse issues, and coauthoring a book on sexual abuse.

JAN HINDMAN, M.S., M.Ed., has extensive experience in the field of child sexual abuse. She was the director of the Incest Treatment Program, Ontario, Oregon, for four years during which time she developed the "restitution" philosophy of sexual abuse treatment. She serves as a consultant to several sexual abuse treatment programs and continues to provide sexual abuse treatment/assessment services in her private practice as well as for the Resti- tution Treatment and Training (RTAT) program. Ms. Hindman is a nationally known lecturer and the author of a number of books and articles on sexual abuse, most notably *A Very Touching Book, Step by Step: Sixteen Steps toward Legally Sound Investigations,* and *Just Before Dawn.*

LUCY HUTCHENS, M.Ed., has extensive experience in child protective services, abuse investigation, and sexual abuse treatment. For the past seven years she has been a Family Sexual Abuse Treatment Specialist in the Oregon Childrens' Services Division, and in that position has served as the coordinator of the RTAT program for five years. A trainer in a number of professional seminars and workshops, she has developed statewide training programs and organized a client peer-counseling network to strengthen the RTAT program.

DENISE McGUIRE, M.A., received her sex-offender treatment training at the Youth Sex Offender Program in Stark County, Ohio. After spending a period of time as a youth sex-offender therapist, she became the program coordinator and has recently returned to graduate school to complete her Ph.D. in psychology.

JAMES M. YOKLEY, Ph.D., is a Clinical Psychologist who has comprehensive psychological evaluation/treatment experience with adults and children. Dr. Yokley, who designed and coordinated the Stark County, Ohio, Youth Sex Offender Program is presently the program's consulting psychologist. In his private practice he continues to provide sexual abuse treatment/assessment services to the program and for the Ohio Department of Youth Services. Dr. Yokley's behavioral assessment/intervention research has been published in a number of professional journals. He has been active in research presentations to professional associations, most recently on the topic of evaluating survivor empathy training procedures for youth sex offenders.

Social Responsibility Statement on Survivor-Offender Communication

Therapists of sexual abuse survivors and sexual offenders have a social responsibility to assure that any survivor-offender meetings conducted are wanted by survivors, safe, therapeutic and do no harm.

Chapter 1
INTRODUCTION TO THE THERAPEUTIC USE OF SURVIVOR-OFFENDER COMMUNICATION

James M. Yokley and Denise McGuire

The use of survivor-offender communication in the treatment of sexual abuse is for some an emotionally charged, value-laden issue. It is not the purpose of this chapter to take a position on whether using survivor-offender communications in the treatment of sexual abuse is morally right. That decision is left up to each individual in sexual abuse treatment who has the right to request or refuse any of the survivor-offender communication interventions described in the three program models presented in this book.

The purpose of this introduction to the therapeutic use of survivor-offender communication is to: (1) acknowledge the current prevalence of survivor-offender communication interventions in the treatment of sexual abuse; (2) list the basic outpatient survivor-offender communication procedures employed along with a summary of their theoretical benefits and their published results; and, (3) describe the guidelines under which the various survivor-offender communication interventions have been used.

The purpose of the other chapters in this book are to present three program models that employ various forms of survivor-offender communication techniques. The various forms of survivor-offender communication interventions described are designed to reinforce the offender's responsibility for the abuse with the hope of helping the survivor's recovery. Survivor safety and well-being are paramount to the implementation of these interventions, none of which should be considered except under carefully controlled conditions.

Prevalence of Survivor-Offender Communication Interventions in the Treatment of Sexual Abuse

A recent national survey of sex-offender programs revealed that 66 percent of the treatment programs surveyed require offenders to apologize to their survivors (Knopp & Stevenson, 1989). Although many sex-offender programs *require* offenders to apologize to their survivors, there is some evidence that both offenders and survivors of serious and violent crimes are *willing* to have apology or mediation sessions.

A Canadian survey by Gustafson (1989) revealed that 87 percent (n=27) of the of- fenders in the study, incarcerated for a variety of serious and violent crimes, indicated that they would choose to meet with their survivors; 10 percent (n=3) "despaired of ever salvaging the familial relationship involved" (p. 8); and three percent (n=l) were philosophically op- posed. The survey indicated that 61 percent (n=17) of the survivors, "even those who had suffered severe trauma, indicated they desired to meet with their offenders, and considered such a meeting to be helpful, if not crucial, to their recovery and ability to put closure on the offence" (p. 9). The other 39 percent (n=11) of the survivors indicated they would choose not to meet their offenders for a variety of reasons.[1]

In another survey conducted after mediation sessions with survivors and offenders of primarily nonviolent crimes (Umbreit, 1990), 97 percent ($\underline{n}$=64) of the offenders stated that apologizing to the survivor was important, while 94 percent ($\underline{n}$=48) of the survivors stated that receiving answers from the offender was important; and 92 percent ($\underline{n}$=47) stated that telling the offender the effect of the crime was important.

The following is a summary of the basic outpatient survivor-offender communication procedures employed, their theoretical benefits, and a review of published results.

Summary of Basic Outpatient Survivor-offender Communication Procedures

Current survivor-offender communication interventions can be classified along two intensity criteria: (1) level of contact - indirect (e.g., writings, recordings, telephone calls) versus direct (i.e., face-to-face communication); and (2) communication source - "objective" (i.e., communications to/from a third party such as unknown survivors or offenders) versus "personal" (i.e., communications by the actual parties involved). These techniques can be further classified according to the intervention setting (i.e., whether they are individual or group procedures). Table 1 illustrates examples of the known range of intensity of survivor- offender individual and group communication interventions currently employed in outpatient settings.

The book chapters include descriptions of the following outpatient survivor- offender communication interventions. The procedures described below are used in *outpatient* offender-treatment programs that generally do not serve rapists who are particularly aggressive and/or physically violent during the course of their offense(s).

Individual Interventions

- Offender apology LETTERS to the Indirect survivors (i.e., significant others to
- the actual survivor) of his/her abuse
- Offender apology SESSIONS involving the INDIRECT survivors of his/her abuse Offender apology LETTERS to the Direct survivors of his/her abuse
- Offender apology SESSIONS involving the DIRECT survivors of his/her abuse Offender therapist telephone contacts with the survivors (or their parents) to keep them informed of the offender's status, and to gather information to be used in the offender's treatment
- Clarification sessions for the offender to "clear up" specific issues of importance to an individual survivor and his/her immediate family
- Clarification scrapbook for the survivor compiled by the offender to "clear up" specific issues of importance to an individual survivor and to be used for future survivor treatment

---

1. According to Gustafson (1989), 2 of the 11 survivors who would choose not to meet with their offenders, "agreed with the concept ... but did not feel it necessary for themselves in the present circumstances". Four indicated, "they would be willing to meet" under other circumstances; two of the four would meet "if the crime had been more serious"; one "if the offender was young and remorseful"; and one if "they as survivors were given more time to recover". Since only five felt they would derive no benefit from a face-to-face meeting with their offender, 82 percent ($\underline{n}$=23) agreed with the concept and under the right circumstances would choose or be willing to meet with offenders.

Table 1
Survivor-offender Communication Interventions by Intervention Setting, Level of Contact, and Communication Source

Individual Interventions

Communication Source	Level of Contact	
	Indirect	*Direct*
Objective	Survivor impact letter to offenders in general	Apology session from the offender to indirect survivor
Personal	Apology letter from the offender to his/her survivor	Apology session from the offender to actual survivor

Group Interventions

Communication Source	Level of Contact	
Objective	Survivor-impact videotape viewed in offender group	Impact group for offenders conducted by survivors
Personal	Police report of crime read in group session	Confrontation of offender by survivor and support group

---

Group Interventions

- Bibliotherapy-assisted survivor-impact understanding groups for offenders (involving news articles, personal letters, and videotape reports by survivors of sexual abuse)
- Survivor-conducted impact groups for offenders
- Offender information groups for survivors (for the offender to "clear up" general issues of importance to the survivor's treatment group)

The procedures listed above do not include all of the survivor-offender interventions currently in practice or any examples of outpatient survivor-offender communication interventions generated by survivor advocates and conducted within the framework of a *survivor* treatment program.[2]

---

2. To the best of our knowledge, other than the traditional survivor-offender apology sessions utilized by survivor therapists prior to family reunification in incest cases and the confrontations of familial offenders by adult survivors of incest (Swink & Leveille, 1986), survivor-offender communication interventions conducted within the framework of a survivor-treatment center has focused on offender confrontations by adult rape survivors. This intervention was developed by the feminist anti-rape movement of the 1970s and early1980s (see Japenga, 1984; and Toronto Rape Crisis Center, 1983, 1986).

Clarification tor Survivor Advocates and Adult Survivors

Since survivor apology sessions are used widely in sex-offender treatment programs (Knopp & Stevenson, 1989), survivor advocates and adult survivors could conclude that survivor-offender communication interventions were constructed by offender-therapists merely to support the offender treatment process, were not sensitive to survivor issues, and therefore would be expected to benefit offenders far more than survivors.

This conclusion would be unfortunate for several important reasons: 1) the historical roots of survivor-offender communication document survivor therapists utilizing offender apology sessions in their incest family reunification cases long before most sex-offender programs adopted that practice; 2) many mental health professionals currently engaged in offender treatment were previously survivor therapists (e.g., the chapter authors in this book) and are currently survivor advocates who either directly emphasize survivor sensitivity or place such a strong emphasis on offender responsibility that survivor sensitivity is inherently developed (see Chapters 2, 3, and 4); 3) apology letters in some offender treatment programs are sent to the *survivor's* therapist, who presents the opportunity to receive an of- fender apology as a part of the *survivor's* (not the offender's) therapy (see Chapter 4); 4) survivors participating in impact panels set up to focus on treatment of the *offender* report positive experiences after their attempts to help offenders understand survivor trauma (see Chapter 4); and 5) the only available case data on the impact of a survivor-offender communication session on an adult survivor of sexual abuse revealed the intervention to be far more beneficial to the survivor than the offender (Drummey, 1990).

Theoretical Benefits of Survivor-offender Communication Interventions

Theoretical Benefits to Survivor Treatment

Some survivor treatment providers have adapted the Kubler-Ross (1969) stages of transition in the process of dying (denial, anger, bargaining, depression, and acceptance) to other severe crises in life. Passage through these stages is viewed as therapeutic in itself for survivor treatment (Mayer, 1983).

Survivors of sexual abuse go through a lengthy and painful recovery process that begins with admitting the problem by identifying themselves as survivors and, for the fortunate, this eventually involves relinquishing the problem and identifying themselves as survivors (Agosta & McHugh, 1987; Figley, 1985; Swink & Leveille, 1986).[3] Survivor recovery involves a process where common problem areas or issues may be worked through in sequence or in a parallel process (Giarretto, 1976). The areas listed below do not include all of the issues that arise in the treatment of sexual abuse but are used as a framework for discussing the potential benefits of various survivor-offender communication interventions.

---

3. "The term 'survivor' is a positive one that connotes strength, growth, and independence" (Mayer, 1985, p. 63) and has been recommended for self-esteem building within the context of treatment.

4

The first area of the recovery process deals with disclosing the secret (Swink & Leveille, 1986) or breaking through denial (Agosta & McHugh, 1987; Giarretto, 1976; McCarthy, 1986). Admitting to being a victim/survivor is often accompanied by self-blame statements which in turn may elicit feelings of guilt. Understanding feeling culpable and the consequent guilt is the second area often addressed by the treatment process (Swink & Leveille, 1986; Agosta & McHugh, 1987; Meiselman, 1978). Successful resolution of these issues involves placing the responsibility for the sexual acts on the perpetrator (Forward & Buck, 1978; Meiselman, 1978), and can often be observed by an increase in anger and rage toward the offender. Healthy expression of this anger is thought to be essential for the survivor if she/he is to proceed through recovery (Agosta & McHugh, 1987; Swink & Leveille, 1986; Giarretto, 1976). Reconsideration (Figley, 1985) or confrontation (Swink & Leveille, 1986) is a point at which the survivor is prepared to confront the trauma and reclaim power. Acceptance (Agosta & McHugh, 1987), adjustment (Figley, 1985), or reintegration (Swink & Leveille, 1986) is a point where the survivor is in recovery and has become a survivor by integrating the sexual abuse into his/her life and using it as a source of strength (Patten, Gatz, Jones, & Thomas, 1989). These survivor skills have been referred to as "self-management" by Giarretto (1976). Through this process, the survivor has developed a positive, stronger sense of self by learning self-acceptance, self-confidence, assertiveness, self-expression of feelings and love" (Swink & Leveille, 1986, p. 140).

Gil (1983) lists a number of cognitive coping mechanisms used by survivors of abuse to tolerate their pain, including minimizing, rationalizing, and selective memory. Theoretically, the use of survivor-offender communication can promote survivor progress in areas where the survivor needs to reintegrate the facts of the offense into his/her understanding of what happened. Potential benefits include: reassurance of the reality of the abuse, relief of guilt- self-blame, appropriate expression of anger, reconsideration of responsibility, and empowerment through confrontation.

Reassurance of the reality of the abuse

Survivor progress with denial might be promoted by providing the survivor with an indirect, personal form of communication about the offender (e.g., a police report showing that the offender confessed to the crime). This type of survivor-offender communication intervention might also help with denial by indirect survivors of the abuse. An indirect, personal communication in the form of a letter to the indirect survivor from the offender, admitting the crime in full detail, may be the only intervention powerful enough to begin to break down the shadows of doubt harbored by the indirect survivor.

In some cases survivor-offender communication interventions may require further presentations and discussion of the material in addition to further time to absorb the offender disclosure.

Relief of guilt/self-blame

Successful resolution of guilt/blame involves placing the responsibility for the sexual acts on the perpetrator (Forward & Buck, 1978; Meiselman, 1978). While it is important for therapists to continue to hold the offender responsible, simply telling child survivors that the sexual abuse was not their fault may reduce their guilt only temporarily and may negate any sense of efficacy the child has experienced (Lamb, 1986).

Progress with the guilt/blame issue might be promoted using an indirect, personal form of survivor-offender communication (written by the actual parties involved), for example, providing the survivor with an apology letter where the offender acknowledged full responsibility for all sexual contact and admitted to forcing, coercing, or otherwise manipulating the survivor into acts against his/her will. Such a communication from an offender may help a survivor begin the process of understanding on a new level that, regardless of what he/she may have been told by the offender or any significant other, the abuse and its aftermath are the offender's fault.

Appropriate expression of anger

The importance of appropriate anger expression is explained by Agosta and McHugh (1987): "It is healthy rage that puts her [the survivor] in touch with her strength and power" (p. 246). Swink and Leveille (1986) similarly note, "Once the rage is released, they regain their power..." (p. 128). The unsent letter is a common treatment technique for survivors of sexual abuse and is considered useful in helping survivors clarify their feelings.

Just as victims of nonviolent crimes report that telling the offender the effect of the crime was important (Umbreit, 1990), sexual crime survivors may also share that need. Sharp (1987) reports the survivors in her care have expressed "a great need to impress upon the offenders how the sexual crimes had impacted on the survivors' lives and the lives of their loved ones" (p. 9). Theoretically, survivor progress with anger expression may be further fostered by implementing a direct, objective communication intervention, such as offering the survivor an opportunity to appear with other survivors to verbally express their feelings as part of a survivor-impact panel before a group of sex offenders in treatment.

Reconsideration of responsibility & empowerment through confrontation

In theory, confronting the truth about the survivor-offender relationship should prompt a reconsideration of the blame/culpability issue. Confrontation of the perpetrator and other involved parties has been referred to as one of the most powerful sexual abuse treatment interventions (McCarthy, 1986).

Swink and Leveille (1986) state, "The purpose of confronting the abuser is not to elicit some expected, hoped-for behavior from him [the offender]; but rather to accomplish some relief for the former survivor, to assert her independence and strength, and to put an end to the old patterns of secrecy, denial, and manipulation" (p. 138). Theoretically, implementing a direct, personal communication intervention, such as offering the survivor an opportunity to participate in survivor-offender sessions, can provide an unparalleled opportunity for the survivor to deal with feelings of anxiety and helplessness by confronting the offender as the source of this emotional turmoil. In cases where the survivor is too young or not yet ready to confront the abuse issue directly, the offender's written admission of responsibility and apology can be compiled with other important data into a scrapbook as an archive for the future treatment of the abuse issue (see Chapter 2).

Survivor progress through the areas outlined above involves the adjustment of attitudes and beliefs as well as the modification of self-statements in order to redirect and learn to manage the affective reactions that have occurred. In theory, much of what was learned might be promoted, enhanced, and a sense of therapeutic closure expedited by the use of various forms of survivor-offender communication.

Theoretical Benefits to Offender Treatment

Important treatment issues to be addressed for offenders include: "cognitive distortions, irrational thinking, or thinking errors which support or trigger offending"; "accepting responsibility for behavior without minimization or externalizing blame"; "development of survivor awareness or empathy" (National Adolescent Perpetrator Network,[4] 1988, p. 28); and providing emotional restitution to the survivor.

Cognitive distortions

The criminal behavior theory that cognitive distortions enable the offender to act out and that cognitive restructuring focused on modifying irrational beliefs or thinking errors are useful in helping the offender with self-control (Douglas, 1989; Yochelson & Samenow, 1977) has been applied to the treatment of sex-offense behavior (Berenson, 1987; Douglas, 1990). The importance of this theoretical approach has been emphasized throughout the report of the National Task Force on Juvenile Sexual Offending (NAPN, 1988).

Since offender cognitive distortions are so ingrained, cognitive interventions (where the offender is asked to become aware of cognitive distortions, consider alternatives, and generate more adaptive thought patterns) may be augmented by the use of survivor-offender communication. Since these interventions bring opinions and facts into therapy that often conflict with the offender's perceptions, survivor-offender communication interventions are expected to strongly reinforce the offender's awareness of cognitive distortions. Thus, theoretically, the use of survivor-offender communication should help intervene with offender cognitive distortions and promote progress through all treatment areas that require that beliefs, attributions, and self-statements be challenged and that situations be re-examined by integrating the actual facts of the offense into the offender's perception of what occurred.

Accepting responsibility

Sex offenders' problems with accepting responsibility directly involve cognitive distortions that range from denial of the abuse to minimizing, justifying, rationalizing, or blaming on others, their situation, or society for the damage they inflicted (Scully & Marolla, 1984). Incest offenders generate similar cognitive distortions as rape offenders (Mayer, 1983). In order to be able to deny complete responsibility for the offense, offenders who molest children may shape or groom their survivors to view themselves as "co-participants" who are responsible for the abuse by requiring the survivor to make a series of choices among various locations, forms, or degrees of abuse, or by choosing a reward.

Having the offender read the survivor-impact statement from the police report or participate in a direct confrontation by the survivor is theoretically helpful in treating the offender's avoidance of accepting total responsibility for the abuse. Offender progress with denial might be promoted by

---

4. Hereinafter referred to as NAPN.

employing an indirect, objective form of communication, such as having the offender read aloud the survivor's statement to the police in his offender treatment group. This intervention would make maintaining denial before an entire group of sex offenders a difficult task.

Offender progress with the blame issue might be promoted using an indirect, personal form of survivor-offender communication (written by the actual parties involved). After sufficient development of survivor-understanding/empathy on the part of the offender, the act of writing an apology letter that acknowledged full responsibility for forcing, coercing, or otherwise manipulating the survivor into sexual acts against his/her will should theoretically reinforce acceptance of responsibility for the offense.

The offender's adjustment and acceptance of the need to change must involve relinquishing thinking errors (Yochelson & Samenow, 1977). Dealing with pride and labeling past behavior as inappropriate is an important step in offender treatment (McCarthy, 1986). Offender adjustment also involves the adoption of a healthy sense of assertiveness and self- disgust about the offense behavior (Yochelson & Samenow, 1977), coupled with self-acceptance as a person who is re-establishing his/her dignity through the development of honesty. Closure on the adjustment and acceptance issue would be expected to be reinforced by direct, personal survivor-offender communication interventions such as apology or clarification sessions.

Survivor awareness or empathy

A lack of survivor empathy enables offending to continue and is considered to be the hallmark of the sexual offender (NAPN, 1988; Sgroi, 1982). A recent national survey reveals that 93 percent of identified sex-offender treatment programs in the United States recognize developing offender empathy for survivors as an important treatment component (Knopp & Stevenson, 1989). Since survivor-offender communication interventions provide information on the thoughts and feelings of others, these interventions have the potential of developing offender empathy (i.e., the understanding of and ability to participate in the thoughts and feelings of others).

To understand the impact of their abusive behavior on others, sex offenders must reconsider their own explanations for such behavior and learn to accept how others interpret it. Reconsideration may be promoted by providing a direct, personal form of survivor-offender communication (i.e., a face-to-face communication spoken by the actual parties involved). In tp.is situation the survivor could be offered a therapy session where she/he could confront the offender, who, in turn, could apologize and accept full responsibility. A "powerful lesson in empathy is learned in survivor/offender sessions" (NAPN, 1988, p. 33).

Survivor-impact understanding (and, in some cases, empathy development) can be further fostered by using a direct, objective form of survivor-offender communication (i.e., face-to-face communication spoken by a third party). This could be accomplished by conducting a survivor-impact session or a survivor-offender group where survivors express their feelings in the presence of sex offenders who are currently in treatment.

Based on her survivor-offender group experiences, Sharp (1987) indicates that for offenders it is "critically important for them to see the survivor's pain, to see the devastating and damaging effects of sexual abuse, and to hear the survivor's cries for wholeness and inner peace" (p. 9). In addition, it is felt that allowing the offenders to see the survivor's anger may help them begin to understand survivor impact. Survivor-offender communication interventions that target survivor empathy may also indirectly help with the offender's blame issue, since offender problems relating to blaming the survivor involve a complete lack of understanding and perception of responsibility.

Confrontation of the offender by the legal system is also considered important in survivor-impact understanding. "Survivor empathy is a trait which offenders do not possess initially. Direct participation in the prosecution process is helpful to the offender. He needs to hear his behavior described as illegal, unacceptable and having an impact on the survivor" (NAPN, 1988, p. 14).

Restitution

The restitution aspect of survivor-offender communications has the potential to provide treatment benefits for both survivors and offenders. In recent years, a major change in juvenile justice has emphasized restitution as a part of treatment or sanction for young offenders in general (McDonald, 1976; Schneider, Schneider, Reiter, & McCleary, 1981; Staples, 1986). In a recent national survey of juvenile-crime survivor-mediation programs, holding the offender accountable was considered the most important mediation goal (Hughes & Schneider, 1989). With respect to restitution to the survivor, court programs most frequently included monetary restitution followed by community service, the combination of monetary restitution and community service, offender behavior requirements (e.g., counseling) and occasionally the return/replacement of property, workshop participation, charitable contributions, and apologies-a form of emotional restitution (Hughes & Schneider, 1989).

Schafer (cited in Staples, 1986) suggests that restitution "is something an offender does, not something done for him or to him and as it requires effort on his part it may be especially useful in strengthening his feelings of responsibility" (p. 180). The potential value to the offender of offering emotional restitution during survivor-offender group sessions was reported by Sharp (1987): "Offenders hoped to influence their own future behavior by talking about what they had done, and in an indirect way, perhaps compensating for their crimes" (p. 9).

Emotional restitution has the potential to address survivor justice ideals while court- ordered restitution has the potential to address initial survivor needs. Some survivors and their advocates have envisioned "real justice" as providing: "money, because that represents the ability to get help; emotional restitution beginning with an apology from the abuser; and open-ended counseling" (Bear & Dimock, 1988, p. 54). Swink & Leveille (1986) report that a few of their adult survivors of childhood incest "are suing their fathers in civil suits to force them to pay for psychotherapy, to expose them as child molesters, and potentially to force them into therapy to stop their abusive behaviors" (p. **129).** As Staples (1986) suggests, "Whether seen as punishing or rehabilitating the offender, restitution seeks, at a minimum, to give some recognition to the claims of the survivor... it also restores the moral balance by making the offender part of the victimization experience" (pp. 179-180). In some cases, seeking validation and retribution through court-ordered restitution can act to promote offender rehabilitation.

Summary of the Published Results of
Survivor-Offender Communication Interventions

The *potential* benefits and other rationales given in theory for attempting survivor- offender communication interventions must be measured against the results of such procedures in practice. Little research has been conducted to indicate what types of communications are safe procedures (i.e., do not cause an adverse impact); no current research exists on what types of survivor-offender communication interventions have the best outcome with different types of survivors or offenders (e.g., age, type or duration of offense, gender, etc.). The limited case study information available is presented below for clinical consideration until such time that empirical research studies on the relative impact of the various survivor- offender communication interventions become available.

Individual Interventions

Writing letters (which may or may not be shared with the therapist and are rarely sent) has been found to be useful in helping survivors discover their emotions (Courtois & Watts, 1982), but may not be sufficient as an intervention to dissipate survivors' affect given the intensity of their emotional trauma (Agosta & McHugh, 1987). On the other hand, reading the survivor letters to *offender* treatment groups has had some impact on their survivor- impact understanding (Yokley, 1989).

Umbreit (1989b) has reported a Survivor-offender Reconciliation Program (VORP) case example involving the rape of a 5-year-old girl by her 13-year-old uncle. This intervention was considered helpful to the mother who initially expressed her readiness to "shoot my brother, kill him" (p. 104) by providing her with the opportunity to confront her brother and work out her anger and hostility towards him while helping him understand the full human impact of his behavior. Umbreit reports that without this intervention the mother probably would not have been able to attend family gatherings where her brother was present.

In another VORP case example, Brenda, a 25-year-old rape survivor, also expressed intense anger and wanted to kill her offender. Although she attempted to channel her emotions in a positive way by starting a rape crisis center, the stress of her trauma took its toll and her marriage failed. After finally trying a VORP mediation session, Brenda stated that before the intervention "I just wasn't a whole person, I felt like a part had been stolen and it had. I didn't know how to get it back, but after the mediation I didn't get that part back but I found a new part that I liked a lot better" (Drummey, 1990). This intervention did not benefit the offender as it did Brenda and he has been incarcerated again for sexual assault.[5]

Other case study results on individual survivor-offender sessions are reported in this book as benefiting the survivors involved by helping increase their emotional expression and decrease

---

5. While Elath (1990) reports reservations of some victim advocates regarding the use of the VORP mediation model in sexual abuse cases, the programs critiqued apparently do not incorporate the kinds of extensive offender and survivor preparation procedures described in this book.

their self-blame attributions about the abuse (see Chapters 2, 3, and 4). In one case study, the psychological testing administered before and after participation in an apology session revealed no adverse impact on the survivor's level of anxiety or helplessness. In addition, a clinical improvement marked by a decrease in level of depression, anger, and unprovoked angry outbursts was noted (see Chapter 4).

Group Interventions

Although survivor-offender group sessions are controversial and require caution, careful planning, and further study, the National Task Force on Juvenile Sexual Offending indicates, "Unrelated survivors report a sense of release and empowerment after confronting an offender other than their own perpetrator in a safe and supportive environment. Offenders often feel their first real remorse after hearing from a survivor other than their own how they feel about abusers" (NAPN, 1988, p. 44). As indicated before, survivor-offender groups have been reported to meet the needs of the survivors "to impress upon the offenders how the sexual crimes had impacted on the survivor's lives and the lives of their loved ones" in addition to finding out what the offender's motivation was, i.e., "Why me?" (Sharp, 1987, p. 9).

Sharp (1987) reports the following results after a single eight-member (plus four group leaders) survivor-offender group session lasting two-and-a-half hours. In follow-up discussions with the rape survivors after the meeting, many said that for the first time in years they were able to not only gain perspective on what happened to them, but also to regain that sense of power and control over their lives that had been stripped from them during the rape. They believed this confrontation, as painful as it was, enabled them to move that much closer to feeling "whole" again (p. 9).

A questionnaire in Chapter 4 of this book revealed that all of the survivors who conducted a Survivor Impact Group (i.e., to help offenders understand the impact of their behavior on others) as well as all of the survivors who participated in an Offender Information Group (i.e., where survivor-requested information about offender behavior is provided by offenders) found these forms of survivor-offender interaction helpful and recommended that other survivors be given the opportunity to confront or speak to offenders in that type of setting. Psychological testing administered before and after survivor participation in these groups revealed no adverse impact on survivors. With respect to impact on the offender, the data indicated that the Survivor Impact Group produced a greater impact on the offenders than any of the other survivor-understanding interventions utilized and had an impact on more variables associated with relapse prevention (see Chapter 4).

While the current results of survivor-offender communication interventions tend to indicate that these interventions hold the potential to promote greater closure and healing in the treatment process, a caution to survivors, offenders, and their treatment providers about raising unrealistic expectations is warranted.

Summary of Guidelines for
Survivor-Offender Communication Interventions

Research-validated standards for conducting survivor-offender communication interventions are not currently available. The following reference material relates to specific professional guidelines for conducting these interventions. This information comes primarily from case studies and is presented as clinical *guidelines* until empirically derived, research- validated standards are developed.

All Survivor-offender Interventions (Individual & Group)
1. Survivor safety

According to the National Task Force on Juvenile Sexual Of- fending, "Adequate precaution must be taken to assure the survivor physical and psychological safety. Survivor/offender sessions should not be attempted until both the survivor and offender therapists are confident that safety can be maintained and the sessions will be beneficial to the survivor's treatment" (NAPN, 1988, p. 30). Safety standards need to be constructed to fit the needs of each treatment program based on the type of survivor-offender communication interventions employed in that program (see Chapters 2, 3, and 4).

2. Survivor choice

Survivor/offender sessions "should always be at the survivor's discretion and entirely voluntary, based on a therapeutic decision in the survivor's best interest" (NAPN, 1988, p. 30). The expansion of the VORP model to violent crimes has brought some suggestions for modification of that program. One important principle was the need to be extremely sensitive to the survivor's feelings and to make sure that a mediation session was scheduled based in the clear choice of the survivor who was not made to feel that such a session "should" be scheduled (Umbreit, 1989). In the interventions described in this book, survivor choice is emphasized and the survivor may terminate the interaction at any time, including immediately before it begins (see Chapters 2, 3, and 4).

3. Participation by selected offenders

Since offenders who have not been in treatment are not likely to show remorse or accept responsibility for their crime (Swink & Leveille, 1986), survivor-offender confrontation sessions with *untreated* offenders are not rec- ommended. In addition, if the abuser is "very violent and vindictive, or completely uncaring, then there would be nothing to gain and too much to risk to confront him" (Swink & Leveille, 1986, p. 129).

4. Careful offender preparation

Sufficient offender preparation should be insured. Careful approaches to the development of the offender's survivor-understanding and sensitivity are required prior to any type of survivor-offender communication (see Chapters 2, 3, and 4). Preparation for this type of intervention may take some time for more serious offenders.

5. Use of responsible, survivor-sensitive language

It is considered important during survivor-offender communication interventions to use "survivor-sensitive" language that holds offenders responsible (see Chapter 3). For example, therapists need to be sensitive to survivor feelings of guilt/culpability by insisting that offenders use "I-statement" phrases expressing their own responsibility (such as, "when I molested him/her," versus "when it happened"). In addition, therapists should avoid presenting topics such as "forgiveness" because they may trigger offender cognitive distortions (e.g., "I was forgiven, so it must not have been all that bad").

6. Professional objectivity

The option to be involved in face-to-face survivor-offender confrontations "should be extended to the individuals concerned, and their decision should be based upon their own needs, not upon a professional's discomfort or biases about survivor-offender meetings" (Sharp, 1987, p. 10).

7. Careful observation and evaluation

The National Task Force on Juvenile Sexual Offending has stated that survivor-offender sessions are controversial and "clearly an area for caution, careful planning, and further study" (NAPN, 1988, p. 44). Therefore, until the various forms of survivor-offender communication are validated as safe and therapeutic through controlled research studies, careful observation and evaluation must be integrated into the clinical use of these methods. Since therapists cannot justify the treatment of one client at the expense of another, it is recommended that programs monitor the impact of the various forms of survivor-offender communication on *both* parties. If possible, it is recommended that survivor and offender affective states as well as cognitive self-statements be evaluated before and after survivor-offender communication interventions are conducted. This evaluation is recommended in order to detect and remediate any adverse impact that might occur as well as to determine the therapeutic value of the interventions. Since psychological defenses or other cognitive coping mechanisms may be active during survivor-offender inter- actions, supplementing self-reports with psychological testing is recommended (see Chapter 4).

Individual Interventions
1. Careful planning and survivor preparation

Survivor-apology sessions involving confrontation of the offender require careful planning. Pre-apology sessions are recommended where such questions as, "How would you feel if your parents/assailant apologized to you and promised to behave differently?" are asked and the survivor's readiness for the confrontation is assessed (Trepper, 1986). During confrontation preparation sessions the survivor clarifies what she/he wants to say and learn, what she/he expects, and what range of possible reactions the offender may show (McCarthy, 1986). These sessions should include rehearsal (role plays) where the survivor can feel safe and supported while preparing to say what she/he wants from the offender in a controlled, calm, assertive manner (McCarthy, 1986; Swink & Leveille, 1986). A fairly comprehensive list of questions that survivors may need to ask themselves before confronting their abusers is provided by Hall (1985). Preparation requirements should be constructed to fit the needs of each treatment program based on the type of survivor-offender communication interventions the program employs (see Chapters 2, 3, and 4).[6]

---

6. A recommended incest case format and sample apology session along with examples of how the therapist coaches the parents and children, clarifies what is being said, and keeps the process on track, is provided by Trepper (1986).

2. Selection factors for survivor participation

Since serious and violent crime survivors "who felt they had been supported from the outset and had received the assistance they needed, seemed more likely to consider the prospect of meeting with the offender" (Gustafson, 1989, p. 8), individuals having received more emotional support may be better candidates to benefit from communication interventions that involve meetings with the offender.

3. Empowering the survivor through offender information

Keeping the survivor informed of the offender's status is recommended to help decrease the survivor's feelings of helplessness (see Chapter 3).

4. Initiation of the intervention in the survivor treatment setting

Apology letters in some offender treatment programs are sent to the survivor's therapist who presents the opportunity to receive an offender apology as a part of the survivor's, not the offender's, therapy. (see Chapter 4).

5. Developing survivor understanding of offender behavior

While survivor understanding components are necessary to offender treatment prior to initiating survivor- offender interactions, once these interactions are underway, promoting survivor understanding of the offender's behavior is also important. For example, Sharp (1987) reported that survivors "desperately wanted to understand why they were raped, what the motivation was and why me?" (p. 9). Therefore, in addition to the offender's taking responsibility for the abuse through an apology, it is recommended that survivor-offender sessions include a component for the offender to "clear up" specific issues of importance to the survivor and/or his/her immediate family (see Chapter 2; also see Chapter 4 for a group example).

6. Apology session timing

It is recommended that survivor-offender apology or clarification sessions be held after the offender has developed adequate survivor understanding/ empathy, yet some time before the end of treatment (see Chapters 2, 3, and 4). This is considered important because in cases where offenders use a "nice guy" image to convey that the offense was not a representation of their true self, their apology may be an attempt to repent and ask forgiveness, "thus making it clear that no further rehabilitation is required" (Scully & Marolla, 1984, p. 541). Thus, these sessions should be offered *before* the actual end of the treatment program so that offenders do not receive a message that completing apology or clarification sessions, issues them a pardon for their offense behavior in the form of a release from treatment.

7. Use of professional staff

A suggested VORP model modification involved the fact that "Victims and offenders involved in crimes of violence are more likely to be in need of more extended counseling and support services than the more typical VORP case ... Rather than trained community volunteers doing the mediation, which is the practice of many VORP projects, more extensively trained and experienced professional mediators will need to be available" (Umbreit, 1989, p. 110). While paraprofessional staff have proven useful in self-help groups such as adult survivor support groups and offender-aftercare support groups (see Chapter 2), given the potential for further

14

trauma to occur, it is recommended that survivor- offender communication interventions be conducted by trained mental health professionals whose. objectivity is not clouded by unresolved survivor/offender issues. In addition, it is considered desirable for the therapist to have experience in working with both survivors and offenders, or to consult directly with another professional who has such experience.

8. Providing an appropriate intervention context
During survivor-offender interactions, it may be helpful to frame the abuse within the larger context of societal oppression of the survivor (see Chapter 3).

Group Interventions
1. Selection factors for survivor participation
Recent group case study data revealed that younger survivors (under age 14) with higher psychological test levels of depression and anxiety were unable to attend the Survivor Impact Session that they had volunteered to conduct (see Chapter 4). Case study data from an Offender Information Group revealed that the youngest survivor in the group (age 14), had the highest anxiety level on her psychological testing and exhibited clinical signs of depression during the group session. Until empirical research findings are available, these data suggest an initial clinical guideline of offering group survivor-offender interventions to survivor volunteers who are older and exhibit fewer or less severe symptoms of depression and anxiety (see Chapter 4).

2. Survivor control of the situation
Survivor panelists conducting a Survivor Impact Group for offenders need to feel safe and in control of the situation. In order to provide that environment, strict offender conduct rules for survivor safety need to be provided. Offender survivor-safety standards (e.g., not sitting next to survivors) along with a behavior contract for offenders that states offender behavior requirements before, during, and after survivor-impact sessions are outlined in this book (see Chapter 4; see Chapter 2 for an individual example).

3. Offender responsibility
Offenders involved in presenting offender information to survivor treatment groups need to be at a level in their treatment where they are able to hold each other clearly responsible and accountable for their abuse. It is recommended that offender-therapists gather the information that survivors want to know about offenders from the survivors themselves rather than controlling the content of the session (see Chapter 4; see Chapter 2 for an individual example).

Summary and Conclusions
The use of survivor-offender communication brings opinions and facts into the treatment setting that often conflict with the perceptions of the survivors and offenders involved. Providing information in treatment that challenges maladaptive self-statements and irrational beliefs is directly relevant to helping survivors and offenders resolve the issues of blame and responsibility for the sexual abuse. Continued acceptance of blame by the survivor and denial of responsibility by the offender increase the possibility of future damage to self or others. Traditional treatment limited to client interactions with the therapist cannot address these damaging beliefs as directly and effectively as survivor-offender communications.

Various types of survivor-offender communication interventions classified according to level of contact and communication source have been suggested as procedures that contribute to the treatment of sexual abuse in individual and group settings. The conditions under which these interventions have been conducted are offered as clinical guidelines until empirically derived standards are developed.

Theoretically, these interventions should provide positive benefits in specific treatment areas for both survivors and offenders. No adverse clinical impact on survivors or offenders as a result of involvement in the various survivor-offender communication interventions de- scribed has been published. Current clinical data on the impact of these interventions has been generally favorable for both survivors and offenders. Although there were more *theoretical* benefits of these interventions for survivors than for offenders and there was some case study evidence of a greater treatment benefit to the survivors involved, no research-validated conclusion on this issue currently exists.

While all of the survivor-offender communication intervention results reported to date reveal no adverse impact or are positive in nature, given the victim advocate concerns about these interventions (i.e., Elath, 1990), a call for more survivor-offender interventions designed to operate within the framework of survivor treatment settings is in order. The need for empirical research studies on the impact of survivor-offender communication interventions is critical. As in the area of sex-abuse treatment in general, "What is desperately needed to help rehabilitative endeavors is objective research by impartial scientists ..."(Mayer, 1988, p. 85). The use of survivor-offender communication interventions will continue to spark emotionally charged debates until the growing body of case studies and research in this area advances to the point where research-validated conclusions on intervention impact are possible.

References

Agosta, C., & McHugh, M. (1987). Sexual assault victims: The trauma and the healing. In T. Williams (Ed.), *Post-traumatic stress disorders: A handbook for clinicians* (pp. 239-251). Cincinnati, OH: Disabled American Veterans.

Bear, E., & Dimock, P. (1988). *Adults molested as children: A survivor's manual for women and men.* Orwell, VT: The Safer Society Press.

Berenson, D. (1987). *Outline of the thinking errors approach: Yochelson's and Samenow's the criminal personality.* Unpublished manuscript.

Courtois, C., & Watts, D. (1982). Counseling adult women who experienced incest in childhood or adolescence. *Personnel and Guidance Journal, 60,* 275-279.

Douglas, W. (1989). RET helpful for inmates. *The Ohio Psychologist, 35(4),* 20-21.

Douglas, W. (1990). RET replaces psychoanalysis in work with sex offenders. *The Ohio Psychologist,* 36(6), 28-29.

Drummey, D. (Producer) (1990). "Criminals meet their victims" in *Real Life with Jane Pauley* (Video). New York: National Broadcasting Company (30 Rockefeller Plaza, New York, NY10012).

Elath, M. (1990). Survivor-offender reconciliation pro- grams: Coming soon to your town? *NCASA News,* Winter 1990, 22-23.

Figley, C. (1985). From victim to survivor: Social responsibility in the wake of catastrophe. In C.R. Figley (Ed.), *Trauma and its wake: The study and treatment of posttraumatic stress disorder* (pp. 70-87). New York: Brunner/ Mazel.

Forward, S., & Buck, C. (1978). *Betrayal of innocence: Incest and its devastation.* Los Angeles: J.P. Tarcher.

Giarretto, H. (1976). The treatment of father-daughter incest: A psychological approach. *Children Today,* 34, 2-5.

Gil, E. (1983). *Outgrowing the pain: A book for and about adults abused as children.* Walnut Creek, CA: Launch Press.

Gustafson, D. (1989). Debunking the myths: Victim- offender reconciliation in serious crime. *Quaker Committee on Jails & Justice Newsletter,* 14(2), 7-9.

Hall, L. (1985). Confrontation. In L. Roberts (1987). *A treatment manual for therapy groups with survivors of childhood incest* (p. 45). Madi- son, WI: The Rape Crisis Center (128 E. Olin Ave. #202, Madison, WI 53713).

Hughes, S., & Schneider, A. (1989). Survivor-offender mediation: A survey of program characteristics and perceptions of effectiveness. *Crime & Delinquency, 35,* 217-233.

Japenga, A. (1984, November 13). Therapy through confrontation with a rapist. *Los Angeles Times,* part V, pp. 1, 8.

Knopp, F.H., & Stevenson, W.F. (1989). *Nationwide survey of juvenile & adult sex-offender treatment programs & models, 1988.* Orwell, VT: The Safer Society Press.

Kubler-Ross, E. (1969). *On death and dying.* New York: MacMillan.

Lamb, S. (1986). Treating sexually abused children: Issues of blame and responsibility. *American Journal of Orthopsychiatry, 56,* 303-307.

Mayer, A. (1983). *Incest: A treatment manual for therapy with victims, spouses and offenders.* Holmes Beach, FL: Learning Publications.

Mayer, A. (1985). *Sexual abuse: Causes, consequences and treatment of incestuous and pedophilic acts.* Holmes Beach, FL: Learning Publications.

Mayer, A. (1988). *Sex offenders: Approaches to under- standing and management.* Holmes Beach, FL: Learning Publications.

McCarthy, B. (1986). A cognitive-behavioral approach to understanding and treating sexual trauma. *Journal of Sex and Marital Therapy,* 12(4), 13-20.

McDonald, W. (1976). Criminal justice and the victim: An introduction. In W.F. McDonald (Ed.), *Criminal justice and the victim* (pp. 17-55). Beverly Hills, CA: Sage Publications.

Meiselman, K. (1978). *Incest: A psychological study of causes and effects and treatment recommenda tions.* San Francisco, CA: Jossey-Bass.

National Adolescent Perpetrator Network (1988). Preliminary report from the national task force on juvenile sexual offending. *Juvenile and Family Court Journal,* 39(2), 5-64.

Patten, S., Gatz, Y., Jones, B., & Thomas, D. (1989). Posttraumatic stress disorder and the treat- ment of sexual abuse. *Social Work, 34,* 197- 203.

Schneider, P.R., Schneider, A.L., Reiter, P.D., & McCleary, C.M. (1981). *Restitution requirements for juvenile offenders: A survey of the practices in American juvenile courts.* Hearing before the Sub-committee on Human Re- sources of the Committee on Education and Labor, House of Representatives, Ninety- seventh Congress, Washington, DC.

Scully, D., & Marolla, J. (1984). Convicted rapists' vocabulary of motive: excuses and justifications. *Social Problems, 31(5),* 530-543.

Sgroi, S. (1982). *Handbook of clinical intervention in child sexual abuse.* Lexington, MA: Lexington Books.

Sharp, D. (1987). Hearing with the heart: Reflections on working with victims and offenders in sexual abuse. *The Quaker Committee on Jails & Justice Newsletter,* 12(2),·9.10.

Staples, W. (1986). Restitution as a sanction in juvenile court. *Crime & Delinquency, 32,* 177-185.

Swink, K., & Leveille, A. (1986). From victim to survivor: A new look at the issues and recovery process for adult incest survivors. *Women & Therapy, 5,* 119-141.

Toronto Rape Crisis Center (circa, 1983). *Principles and practice of confrontation.* Toronto: Toronto Rape Crisis Center (P.O. Box 6597, Station "A", Toronto, Ontario, Canada M5W 1X4).

Toronto Rape Crisis Center (1986). *Three alternatives to the legal system.* Toronto: Toronto Rape Crisis Center (P.O. Box 6597, Station "A", Toronto, Ontario, Canada M5W 1X4).

Trepper, T. (1986). The apology session. *Journal of Psychotherapy and the Family, 2,* 93-101.

Umbreit, M. (1989). Crime victims seeking fairness not revenge: Toward restorative justice. *Federal Probation,* September, 52-57.

Umbreit, M. (1989b). Violent offenders and their victims. In Wright, M. & Galaway, B. *Mediation and Criminal Justice* (p. 100-112). London: Sage Publications.

Umbreit, M. (1990). *Program evaluation report: Center for victim offender mediation (calendar year 1989).* Unpublished manuscript.

Yochelson, S., & Samenow, S. (1977). *The criminal personality,* (Vols. 1-3). New York: Jason Aronson.

Yokley, J.M. (1989, April). *An evaluation of four procedures used to develop victim empathy in youth sex offenders.* Paper presented at the conference of the Ohio Coalition for the Treatment of Adolescent Sex Offenders, Co- lumbus, OH.

Chapter 2
THE RESTITUTION MODEL: THE RESTITUTION TREATMENT AND TRAINING PROGRAM

Jan Hindman and Lucy Hutchens

Abstract

This treatment program is based on a restitution model with a strong victim orientation integrating victim restoration with offender treatment. The treatment approach uses clarification meetings between the victim and the offender to help the victim work through present problems as they occur. A clarification is not an apology that emphasizes emotional restitution. A clarification is an offender explanation of his/her manipulative behavior with no attempt to elicit sympathy or forgiveness from the victim. In addition, a treatment scrapbook created by the offender to help with the victim's current treatment can be used to address future problems if/when they occur. The developmental needs of the victim are paramount: clarification sessions are conducted in age-appropriate language, and both overt harm and covert distortions are addressed and remediated. The victim is empowered by choice, by experiencing adult respect from the offender and support people, and by being visible as a person in the eyes of the offender. The offender-treatment program involves close cooperation with the courts, polygraph and plethysmograph assessments, and mandated educational components. The opportunity for the offender to regain self-respect and continue restitution by becoming a volunteer peer-counselor is provided.

Introduction and Treatment Philosophy

The Restitution Treatment and Training (RTAT) program evolved from services offered by the Malheur County Interagency Abuse Team in 1980. Until reorganization as a private nonprofit entity in 1985, the program was housed in the county's mental health clinic, serving a vast geographical area of Eastern Oregon with a scattered population of approximately 30,000 people.

The program was originally designed for adult incest offenders and members of their immediate families, and the language of this chapter reflects that origin. Due to the rural nature of the county, and because of its limited resources, however, the program gradually broadened to include all sexual victims and perpetrators who could benefit from the RTAT approach.

Currently, 265 individuals in 21 peer groups are involved in various levels of treatment. Any sex offender who is assessed as an appropriate risk for outpatient treatment and has some financial, emotional, or psychological restitution to offer his/her traumatized victim(s) can be accepted into the RTAT program. Overtly violent offenders and stranger- rapists are therefore not considered appropriate for acceptance. All victims are treated within the program, and some form of problem clarification or scrapbook (as outlined in the Treatment Description and detailed in Phase 3 below), is implemented even when an offender is not available.

Program Philosophy

Although attitudes and approaches to treatment have changed over the years, three essential components of the RTAT program continue to undergird its victim-oriented philosophy:

1. *The welfare of children* is the paramount consideration;

2. *Interagency cooperation* is absolutely essential when resources are scarce or nonexistent;[1]
3. *Peer involvement* is the only way to avoid professional burn-out and give treated family members the type of ongoing personal growth experiences that may interrupt the familial cycle of abuse.

RTAT program philosophy is based on the belief that victimization occurs on four levels: *child, family, community, and society.* Rather than paying for the crimes of sexual offenders through expensive incarceration followed by parole (which may not include treatment and thus may threaten the safety of the community or the victim), Restitution Treatment involves the offender in treatment to learn how to control and correct his aggressive sexual behavior and gives the offender the opportunity to pay emotional, psychological, and financial restitution to victims at all four levels.

The program strives to find a middle ground which can address the concerns of helping professionals who emphasize victim advocacy and prosecution, as well as the concerns advanced by the proponents of a non-prosecutorial family systems approach. RTAT propounds a logistical organization of "when" these different modalities are used.

RTAT recognizes that a crime has been committed and should be prosecuted to the full extent of the law. However, it also recognizes that the court process may be damaging to children and all effort should be made to offer the sex offender an opportunity for treatment in exchange for a *guilty* plea.

RTAT is based on the belief that "change" or rehabilitation for sex offenders is divided into two stages. First, the offender must be motivated in order for the second step of change to occur. Following the motivation phase, therapy involves (1) learning about the sexual abuse problem, (2) unlearning power-abusive patterns, and (3) relearning new ways of dealing with self/others. Without the "motivation" provided by the intervention of the criminal justice system, learning, unlearning, and relearning will be ineffective and may actually encourage recidivism.

Since children are forever psychologically attached to their families, RTAT upholds the importance of families in the therapeutic process. The family unit, and the offender as an important, powerful part of that unit, hold the potential to repair the emotional damage to victims.

The RTAT model proposes at a certain point in treatment that an offender can earn the "privilege" of being involved in traditional, humanitarian, trusting therapy. At the same time, RTAT believes that the criminal aspects of the offender's behavior must never be forgotten and must always continue to provide the motivation for the offender's continual growth and avoidance of relapse.

---

1. The Interagency Abuse Team developed a protocol (15 pages) outlining the responsibilities of each agency involved in child sexual abuse cases. This step-by-step process has been re-examined and changed through the years and is included in the *Restitution Treatment and Training Program Manual,* available from RTAT, P.O. Box 800, Ontario, OR 97914, (503) 889-3910.

Treatment Description

The treatment process for the sex offender is divided into four phases with clearly delineated goals and expectations, described below. The requirements in Phases 1 and 2 must be completed before the offender can begin work on the most important task of preparing a *clarification presentation* and a *scrapbook* for the victim. The clarification presentation and scrapbook are designed to remove the burden of guilt from the victim by getting the offender to "clear up" exactly what he did to cause all of the problems that the family is experiencing. The scrapbook, which provides a written record of the offender's problem (what happened, how it happened, and why), is also useful for future therapy with the victim.

The clarification to the victim and family members is considered *emotional restitution* for the child and the family. Financial restitution is an ongoing offender responsibility throughout primary and aftercare treatment phases for the offender, the victim(s), and the rest of the family members. Finally, the offender can begin to make restitution to the community in the Aftercare of Phase 4 by providing support services to people involved in the RTAT program and to society in general by ensuring his/her continued personal growth and avoidance of hurtful behavior and thinking patterns.

Phase 1

The first phase begins with legal intervention and ends with the acceptance of the offender into treatment. The "spirit" of Phase 1 is that probation is a privilege and that the offender must make an effort to be accepted. Intervention must be swift, coordinated, and governed by the sexual abuse team protocol.[2] Emotional protection of the victim is the primary concern.

When a sexual abuse complaint is received, a joint investigation is initiated by the child protection worker and the appropriate law enforcement agency and is conducted according to a specific protocol designed to be legally sound in court.[3] After interviewing the child, the investigative team determines whether the complaint is valid and "orchestrates" further investigation plans so that the nonoffending parent can be interviewed away from the alleged offender and without his knowledge. This is done in order to influence the nonoffending parent to be emotionally supportive of the child. At times this means that the child protection worker will interview the nonoffender alone, while the police officer makes arrangements to interview the alleged offender.

Peer-counseling by volunteers from Act 2 (the Aftercare treatment phase) is pro- vided to both the victim and the nonoffending parent. Act 2 volunteers are individuals who have completed primary treatment and have participated in special program training, both formal and informal, in order to give crisis intervention and support to members of new RTAT families throughout the legal process. Offender-volunteers talk to new offenders, volunteer spouses of offenders are matched with spouses of new offenders, etc.

---

2. See footnote 1.
3. See Hindman, J. (1987). *Step-by-step: Sixteen steps toward legally sound sexual abuse investigations.* Available from AlexAndria Associat.es, 911 S.W. 3rd Street, Ontario, OR 97914, (503) 889-8938.

Peer-counselors are selected from Aftercare (Act 2, Phase 4) volunteer clients by the RTAT program coordinator and other professional members of the RTAT treatment team. Basic crisis intervention, interviewing, and group facilitation training is provided in both a formal class and an informal "on the job" basis. These volunteers[4] operate in pairs, with a more experienced individual teamed with one less experienced. This is especially important with offenders who tend to take too much control without peer-monitoring.

A peer-counselor lay coordinator is available to law enforcement and other professionals to refer appropriate peer-counselors according to the situational need. The lay coordinator, often with professional advice, attempts to match new family members with peer-counselors who had similar offense and family situations. It is most important that the peer-counselors be given as much information as possible before making contact with new family members.

Guidelines that serve as a basis for training peer-counselors appear in Appendix A.[5] *Project Pyramid,* a manual containing basic sexual abuse information and facilitation skills for volunteers is also used in the formal training.[6]

Peer-counseling is also offered to the alleged offender if this appears to the investigator to be a helpful resource. Experience indicates that this is important to facilitate *before* a defense lawyer becomes involved. The particular Act 2 peers assigned to a new family are selected and coached by the program coordinator according to the perceived needs of the new family (see Appendix A).

The investigative team members determine whether the nonoffending parent can be emotionally supportive to the child and can protect the child from the offender. The alleged offender is advised to leave the home and the nonoffending parent is assured that the child will remain in the home as long as the offender is not there. Temporary custody and shelter placement for the child victim is only sought if necessary to her/his emotional or physical welfare.

An oral report is made at the next meeting of the interagency team, and a written police report is prepared for the district attorney. If the district attorney makes the decision to proceed, the grand jury is presented with the case as soon as possible in order to avoid a preliminary hearing, an omission permissible under Oregon law. It is also possible for the offender to choose to waive his right to the grand jury process if he plans to plead guilty.

The grand jury process enables the prosecutor to evaluate the ability of the child to be successful in a public trial. Use is made of the fact that the defense attorney has not seen the child testify and plea bargain offers are made or considered accordingly.

After a grand jury indictment, the offender is arrested, arraigned, and usually released under the condition that (1) he/she will have no contact with *any* minor children (not just the victim) and,

---

4. In Oregon, these volunteers may be certified by the state-operated Volunteer Services Program. State liability insurance can cover such individuals while on assignment, since, in the RTAT geographical area, driving is often necessary.

5. The development and implementation of this program component can be found in the RTAT program manual, see footnote #1.

6. See Hindman, J. (1984). *Project pyramid.* Available from RTAT, see footnote 1.

(2) the offender may investigate the possibility of admission to the RTAT program without future legal consequences as a result of those inquiries. Imposition of the no-contact order also removes the burden from the nonoffending spouse of choosing between the offender and the victim.

If the accused offender chooses to investigate admission to the RTAT program, team members. from RTAT and the Act 2 peer-counselor volunteers attempt to engage the individual and his/her spouse in orientation and intake sessions. The alleged offender may attend two sessions of the primary offender treatment group before making a plea decision. At no time during the orientation or informational gathering process is the alleged offender required to discuss his/her situation. The alleged offender is allowed to investigate all aspects of the local treatment program without self-incrimination.

If the offender's decision is to request entrance into the RTAT program, he/she must first enter a guilty plea to a sexual abuse crime and must sign the treatment contract and follow those rules even before being officially accepted and sentenced.[7] The RTAT evaluation is requested as part of the court-ordered presentence investigation completed by a state parole and probation officer. During this four-to-six-week process, the offender is permitted to continue attending the weekly treatment group but is not permitted to participate fully until formally sentenced and the treatment is part of his/her probation requirements.

RTAT evaluation includes a physiological assessment (using the penile plethysmograph) and considers the offender's risk to relapse in an outpatient setting. Most importantly, the evaluation examines the contribution the offender may be able to make in repairing the emotional damage to the victim.

The victim and affected family members are encouraged to become involved in treatment groups immediately. They are accepted into the ongoing program regardless of the perpetrator's decision.

If the offender chooses to plead not guilty, the victim and family are prepared for the court process. They receive the ongoing support of the Act 2 peer-counselors, the RTAT- employed victim advocate, and a Victim Witness Advocate employed by the district attorney's office.

If, after subjecting a child to a public trial, the offender is found guilty, he will not be accepted into the RTAT program until he has experienced a significant jail consequence and admits guilt for a sexual abuse crime.

---

7. See the RTAT program manual, availability noted in footnote 1.

Phase 2

This phase is designed to change the thinking of the offender, to teach compliance with the offender contract, and to establish an open and honest relationship with the therapist via successful completion of a polygraph examination covering the offender's self-reported sexual history. The county district attorney grants immunity to offenders for any crimes committed previous to acceptance into the program, provided the offender successfully completes the program. For the victim and affected members of the family, Phase 2 focuses on strengthening positive family dynamics to recognize and compensate for the inequitable power and control systems imposed by the offender.

The RTAT model recommends that offenders be placed on a work-release type of incarceration to validate the fact that they have committed a crime, while still being required to support themselves and their families and to pay for their treatment. Currently, due to jail overcrowding, the circuit court generally imposes on the offender electronic surveillance and informal house arrest for a short time prior to his/her being permitted more freedom in the community.

At the first treatment group following sentencing, offenders are given a *New Group Member Packet.*[8] Included are assignments that assure complete understanding of the con- tract; develop awareness of "thinking errors";[9] and provide instructions for the preparation of thinking error logs and regular reports on any accidental contact with minors.

In addition to working on an understanding of distorted cognitions, the offender's therapy focus for the first three-to-six months is on the preparation of a complete sexual history followed by a polygraph examination regarding the offender's history and compliance with probation rules. Success in the polygraph examination can enable the offender to proceed to Phase 3, while failure can mean a return to the beginning of Phase 2. Additionally, failure may return the offender to court for consideration of probation revocation or other consequences.

If results of the physiological assessment (penile plethysmograph) during the Phase 1 evaluation indicates a discriminate pattern of deviant sexual arousal, an aversive conditioning plan is developed during Phase 2[10] as a parallel treatment component. (If the offender demonstrates an "indiscriminate" arousal pattern typical of incest offenders-the statistical majority within the RTAT Program-aversive conditioning is postponed until Phase 4.) The Sexual Arousal Control group, a six-month individualized behavioral conditioning course, including both aversive conditioning and fantasy work, is completed in both group and individual settings. Three penile plethysmograph assessments are administered over this period to assist the offender in learning how to control inappropriate arousal. The Sexual Arousal Control component may be completed in conjunction with other Act 2 group or growth component offerings.

---

8. See the RTAT program manual, footnote 1.
9. "Thinking errors" were first described by Yochelson and Samenow (1976-77). *The criminal personality,* Vol. I & II. Dunmore, PA: Jason Aronson, Inc.
10. Offenders with more deviant arousal patterns will have participated in a parallel aversive conditioning program throughout *all* of the first three phases of treatment. Individual evaluations determine the need for this additional behavioral therapy previous to Act 2, Phase 4.

Simultaneously with the offender's therapy work, a trauma assessment[11] of the victim is completed. A trauma assessment of the nonoffending spouse is included, particularly if the spouse is an unresolved child molestation victim. Treatment plans are completed in conjunction with pre-clarification group therapy sessions. The group therapists meet in weekly staff meetings to coordinate the treatment plan.

The most difficult concept for family members to understand and for victims to accept is the "no-contact" restriction. For the family, this restriction is compared to incarceration and it is made clear that the system, not the direct therapists, is responsible for this decision. Limited contact may occur between the nonoffending spouse and the offender, *provided the emotional needs of the victim and other children are of primary consideration.* Also, victims and siblings may, *at their request,* have one-way contact with the offender through the offender's therapist. This process allows items such as cards, letters, or gifts to be given from the children without reciprocity allowed from the offender.

Phase 3
- *Phase 3 involves a process whereby the offender works toward repairing the emotional damage to the victim and to affected family members. By successfully completing Phase 2, the offender earns the privilege of receiving the instructions for preparing the clarification. If violations occur or lack of cooperation is observed, the offender can lose the privilege of working toward the clarification goal and be returned to Phase 2.*
- *The clarification is neither an apology nor a letter of responsibility. It is a carefully designed process to clarify and resolve for the victim what happened. Additionally, this process gives the offender the ultimate opportunity to change his/her thinking and proceed toward acquiring sensitivity and empathy.*

Anticipating the completion of the clarification which will place the full burden of responsibility on the offender is a rehabilitative experience for the victim and other family members. All arrangements and procedures governing the clarification presentations are chosen by the victim(s) and family, thus serving to empower those previously manipulated by the offender.

The victim's scrapbook is a compilation of the offender's written clarification along with supportive letters and pictures from family members and other individuals involved in dealing with the child's abuse. It provides the vehicle whereby the abuse is objectified and can be reviewed in the future when memory may obliterate or confuse some of the facts.[12] Although scrapbooks tend to vary from case to case, each contains the following information: a description of the child, an assessment of the trauma, and complete explanations of what happened, how it happened, and why it happened.[13]

---

11. For information on the trauma assessment see Hindman, J. (1989). *Just before dawn: From the shadows of tradition to new reflections in trauma assessment and treatment of sexual 11ictimization.* Available from AlexAndria Associates, see footnote 3.
12. "RTAT trauma assessment data, gathered over the past 10 years, indicate that those children who are able to separate the sexual abuse from normal sexual development have the greatest opportunity for recovery.
13. Scrapbook philosophy and process is available from AlexAndria Associates, see footnote 3.

After receiving the clarification assignments, the offender proceeds through specific steps in the clarification process including verbal presentations in the treatment group, video presentations, and written attempts for the scrapbook. These components are perused, evaluated, and critiqued until the therapists believe the offender can honestly explain to the child what happened, and answer questions in a way that removes any burden of guilt from the victim. A brief outline of each clarification component and rationale for these components appear in Appendix B.

The offender is then permitted to write a letter requesting permission to meet with the nonoffending parent(s). If a meeting is arranged, the offender will present the clarification components to the parent as they will be presented to the victim, and then asks permission to present the material to the child.

If parental permission is granted, the victim is consulted and given choices regarding participation in the clarification. Creative, encouraging therapy and peer-group discussions are crucial in assisting the child to accept and use some power and control in making the decision and creatively setting limits.

If the victim agrees to listen, the offender presents the clarification, proceeding through each carefully designed component. This process may take several meetings and it continues until all questions have been answered and all family members have participated.

Presentation of the scrapbook is usually made some time after completion of the actual in-person sessions. This is done in a therapeutic setting with the child being given lots of time to read the contents and to discuss the contributions from friends, family, and professionals. If the child is too young to comprehend the scrapbook material, it is presented to a parent with suggestions regarding its use in the future.

RTAT counselors have found that the clarification scrapbook can serve as a thera-peutic "archive for the future" for those victims who need further clarification work later in their lives as well as for those who are unable to receive, or are prevented from receiving, an "in-person" clarification-resolution process with the offender. Recently, an 18-year-old victim, whose mother had refused to permit her to participate three years previously, contacted the program and requested to see her scrapbook. She appeared to receive an overwhelmingly positive understanding of her victimization from the presentation and explanation of the scrapbook that her offender left for her.

After successful completion of the clarification, contract rules regarding family visits and contact with minors may be modified on an individual basis, with the comfort of the victim and family as the prime consideration. Generally, family contacts resume at Act 2 (the Aftercare phase) meetings, which the offender is mandated to attend following completion of Phase 3. The general rule is that the offender may have contact with minors if a responsible adult is present.

Phase 4

- *Phase 4 involves participation in a variety of Act 2[14] (Aftercare) classes, groups, and activities. Act 2 provides a supportive climate in which to encourage ongoing personal growth and strengthening of interpersonal relationships. This phase also serves the monitoring purpose of- (1) ensuring the protection and safety of family members, (2) encouraging the ongoing personal progress of the offender, and (3) ensuring the community's safety.*
- *Offenders are mandated to complete five "growth components," including 12-week classes in Human Sexuality, Effective Parenting, Interpersonal Communication Skills, Personal Development, and an intensive six-month involvement in a Sexual Arousal Control group (teaching an individualized behavioral conditioning approach for the control of inappropriate sexual arousal).*

Most offenders in the RTAT program receive five years of probation and spend an average of 12-to-18 months preceding through the first three phases. Offenders and their families remain in Phase 4 for the remainder of probation, after which they are encouraged to remain voluntarily as peer-counselors. These committed "volunteers" are the program's great source of strength and have been instrumental in its survival.[15]

During Act 2 involvement a family can be assisted in making a decision about reunification. It has been possible in some cases for couples to decide *not* to resume their marriage, but to continue to be involved in the program in a positive way.

Ongoing support groups include *Offenders, Nonoffending Spouses and Parents, Adult Survivors, Act 2 Teens, Act 2 Preteens, Spanish Speakers, Self-esteem for Kids* (child care component), and *Crisis Support* (see Appendix C). A *Couples Group* is provided whenever couples' issues are not being addressed in one of the growth component classes.

Self-esteem and leadership skills are developed with participation by mandated or nonmandated offenders, spouses, nonoffending family members, and adult victims as elected officers or committee members in the Act 2 business meetings. Act 2 leaders are involved in activities that focus on providing peer support, assist the treatment program, and promote public awareness about the problem of child sexual abuse.[16] Classes in peer-counseling skills are offered on a regular basis, and may last from one-to-twelve sessions. The orientation for new offenders and spouses is completed with the participation of Act 2 members in a small group setting led by a professional.

RTAT arranges for quarterly polygraphs; while the offender *must* take a minimum of two polygraphs per year throughout his/her probation, additional polygraphs are required if violations are reported or if the last test indicated deceptive or inconclusive results. It is possible for an offender to be "demoted" to an earlier phase of treatment if warranted by deterioration in progress or

---

14. Act 2 stands for "After care treatment• and is similar to traditional therapy within the family systems model. Act 2 was patterned after the Parents United Program in San Jose, California and was a Parents United chapter from 1981 until the program's reorganization in 1985.
15. For example, in 1985, when the treatment program needed extensive reorganization and volunteer time to deal with its financial collapse, the Act 2 organization donated its entire treasury of $1,000 to the effort. This purchased the phones and bookkeeping system for RTAT.
16. Details on Act 2 organization are included in the RTAT manual, see footnote 1.

contract violations. This is decided by consensus of the interagency team members and the probation officer. Execution of the original sentence is always possible, generally during Phase 2 but rarely at the Phase 4 level.

Participants in Act 2 have the opportunity to learn new skills for living productive lives, specifically how to interact positively with family members, become child-centered, and learn how safely to have a good time.

Approximately 10 offenders have continued to participate voluntarily after the end of their probation. One of the Parents United/Act 2 "founding couples" is still heavily involved in crisis intervention activities. Another offender-volunteer serves as a group facilitator and is recognized as a paraprofessional staff member.

RTAT treatment process goals and treatment activities conducted during each phase of the program are summarized in Tables 1 and 2.

Case Study

George, a 35-year-old white male, was arrested for sexual abuse in the first degree regarding the five-year molestation of his daughter, Susie, age nine. George was employed as a supervisor in a large manufacturing plant. He was a respected member of the church and community and was clearly the head of the household. George is attractive and educated, as well as socially and verbally competent. His wife·, Mary, is also educated and attractive, with a history of childhood sexual abuse. Susie has an older sister, age 11, an older brother, age 14, and two younger siblings, ages 2 and 7.

In Phase 1, at initial evaluation, George reluctantly admitted his five-year sexual involvement with Susie. His victim contact culminated with behaviors of cunnilingus, fellatio, and attempted intercourse during the 18 months prior to discovery. Susie's report to a teacher was accidental and George denied his involvement for approximately 10 days. After confrontation by his wife and the reality of control from the system, George admitted a problem. However, there remained grave discrepancies between his accounts of what occurred and Susie's report to the police and Child Protective Services.

In Phase 1, during his penile plethysmograph evaluation, George demonstrated an "indiscriminate" arousal pattern typical for incest offenders-showing arousal patterns to both children and adults along with an inability to discriminate between violent and consenting scenarios. George's history also included admissions regarding the sexual abuse of two of his sisters during adolescence as well as engaging in extramarital affairs. George denied being sexually abused as a child.

During Phase 2, the relationship perspective of Susie's trauma assessment indicated that Susie had very little ability to view herself as the victim and her father as the perpetrator. Susie was very attached to her father and recognized that the dynamics in the family, as well as in the community and church, projected positive attributes toward her father. These factors prohibited

Table 1 RTAT Treatment Process Summary Chart: Treatment Goals	
Phase 1	**Goals**
Offender	1. Submit a guilty plea 2. Accept treatment 3. Receive probation with some consequences
Family	1. Emotional protection of victim (avoidance of placement) 2. Emotional support for nonoffending family members
Phase 2	**Goals**
Offender	1. Establish honest relationship with therapists 2. Change offender thinking 3. Internalize/accept all contract rules 4. Pass polygraph on sexual history
Family	1. Strengthen family dynamics 2. Recognize how offender controlled them 3. Use trauma assessments to assist family members in understanding how the offender damaged the victim
Phase 3	**Goals**
Offender	1. Clarification presentations 2. Completion of Victim Scrapbook 3. Change offender thinking - acquisition of sensitivity and empathy
Family	1. Alleviate victim/family guilt 2. Placement of all burden of responsibility on offender
Phase 4	**Goals**
Offender	1. Prevent recidivism 2. Maintain changes in thinking
Family	1. Continue personal growth and self-esteem 2. Strengthen family dynamics 3. Reunification decision 4. Continue participation and contribution of time to program as peer supporters

Susie from adopting an "innocent" role. Susie was saddened by lack of contact with her father and post-disclosure issues indicated Susie saw herself as the "perpetrator" for making the report.

The developmental perspective of the trauma assessment (see Appendix D) indicated Susie was in the extremely critical "unfortunate" stage of development. When the abuse started, Susie was in a previous stage of development. In her "un- aware" stage she often cooperated, acquiesced, and perhaps even initiated some of the sexual contact with her father. At age nine, she was proceeding developmentally and was examining the significance of her involvement. Additionally, Susie was taking steps toward developing her arousal system and recognizing society's view of

Table 2
RTAT Treatment Process Summary Chart: Treatment Activities

Phase 1 Activities
1. Investigation conducted according to Team Protocol
2. Peer support available to all family members
3. Preparation of victim/family for legal process
4. Grand Jury indictment - arrest - arraignment
5. Release agreement- no contact with minors, leave home, may investigate treatment program without prejudice
6. Guilty plea- offender evaluation and penile plethysmograph ordered as part of presentence investigation
7. Not guilty plea- victim and family are supported and prepared throughout trial process

Phase 2 Activities: *Offender*
1. Completion of any legal consequences
2. Receipt of *New Group Member Packet*
3. Prep of all assignments and sexual history (pass polygraph on sexual history)
4. Initiate own participation in group
5. Acceptance and responsibility for all financial obligations

Phase 2 Activities: *Family*
1. Participation in peer groups
2. Ongoing peer support
3. Arrangements/completion of all indicated trauma assessments

Phase 3 Activities: *Offender*
1. Verbal/written clarification preparation in group via written scrap- book attempts, videos, ongoing critiques
2. Collect scrapbook materials
3. Continue polygraph monitoring

Phase 3 Activities: *Family*
1. Therapeutic work on feelings
2. Ongoing review of findings in trauma assessment
3. Discuss possible questions for clarification
4. Consider Clarification choices & decisions (whether or not to hear it, physical arrangements, etc.)

Phase 4 Activities: *Offender*
1. Gradually increase contact with minors
2. Polygraph monitoring throughout probation (minimum of two per year)
3. Complete aftercare requirements: *sexual arousal control,* classes in *human sexuality, parenting, communication,* and *personal development* (see Appendix C)
4. Resolution of childhood victimization
5. Acceptance of leadership opportunities, participation in peer-counseling classes, experiences and public awareness-abuse prevention techniques

Phase 4 Activities: *Family*
1. Involvement in ongoing peer support groups
2. Participation in leadership, personal growth activities

sexuality. Without immediate intervention and treatment, the sexually deviant acts committed upon her by her father would become the foundation of her sexual future and she would continue to be damaged developmentally.

The situational portion of the trauma assessment evaluated the victim's potential for phobic reactions and cognitive distortions. Susie's description of the sexually abusive scene provided information indicating that the abuse had been extensive. In that scene, many of the elements, such as conversation, manipulation, and intimidation, provided Susie with information that would further separate her from being innocent in the abusive scenario. There appeared to be tremendous potential for phobic reactions and for the distorted view of being "damaged goods" to develop if a resolution did not occur. For example, George told Susie, "Because I love you so much, Susie, I won't tell your mom about the touching you did to me."

In the six months following discovery and arrest, George was sentenced, received community service as a consequence and entered into Phase 2 of treatment.

Prior to his first polygraph, George added three additional victims to his sexual history, two of whom were stepchildren from a previous marriage. However, his polygraph examination indicated deception and George admitted that he withheld discussing inappropriate fondling and fellatio of his youngest son during the child's infancy, as well as two violations of" accidental contact" with children in a restaurant. Although RTAT offenders are granted immunity from prosecution for any crimes committed previous to their arrest, George chose to withhold this information until the polygraph. As a result of his dishonesty, George was incarcerated for five days, lost the privilege of working on his clarification, and remained in Phase 2 until a successful polygraph was completed three months later.

In the ninth month of treatment, George entered Phase 3 and began work- ing on clarification. During the 14 months of his clarification preparation, two more minor violations of his treatment contract occurred. His unreported contact with a minor and his unexcused absence from the group resulted in an additional ·court appearance and a subsequent term of community service. George also received a sentence of four weekends in the county jail due to his noncompliance before he was finally able to present his clarification to his wife Mary.

The following clarification "Description" (see Appendix B for an explanation of clarification components) was written by George about his daughter's unique and positive attributes:

> Susie, one of the special things about you is that you are the kind of little girl who always had a good attitude and always smiles. I remember at Christmas time, at Grandma Ida's house, when everyone had opened their presents, you wanted to keep everybody happy. You would run around the living room and wrap the presents back up so that your brother Brandon and sister Missy could open them all over again. You even wrapped one for Old Uncle Bert! You weren't interested in playing with your own toys or being selfish, you wanted everyone to be happy and for everyone to have the same smiles Susie had. You would wrap all the presents back up so that we could all have the fun of opening them again.
>
> I also remember another time when you had an especially good attitude. I remember when we were taking Franko, the cat, to Dr. Applegate because he was sick. Franko was sitting in your lap and you had on your yellow dress with the green buttons. Franko wasn't feeling very well and he threw

31

up all over your pretty dress. Even though it was yucky and awful, you kept smiling and petting Franko. You just kept petting Franko and he appreciated you, even though he kept burping. That's one of the very special things about you, Susie. No matter how yucky things are, no matter if everyone else is sad, you always smile and have a good attitude.

George wrote the following clarification on "How" (see Appendix B) he misused his daughter's positive qualities:

Susie, one of the ways I was able to do secret touching to you and keep it a big secret in our family was that I knew you tried so hard to have a good attitude. When I did secret touching to you, it was yucky for you. I made you do things that you didn't want to do. I tricked you. It was very yucky. One of the ways I was able to do this was that I knew Susie would always be smiling and always tried to have a good attitude even if things were yucky. Other kids are sometimes brats and don't care about happy things or keeping everyone else in the family happy like you do. Some little girls think only about themselves. I knew you were the kind of little girl who wanted things to be happy in the family. I knew you were someone who had a good attitude even if things were yucky. That's one of the ways that I could do secret touching to you. I knew that I could do yucky things and Susie would keep her good attitude and not tell.

Susie, I want you always to know that being a happy kid and having a good attitude is wonderful. You should be proud of yourself and keep that good part forever and ever. There is nothing wrong with having a good attitude when things are yucky. There is only something wrong with people like me who trick little girls who have good attitudes.

On George's clarification of the "Trauma Assessment" (see Appendix B) of his daughter, he wrote:

Susie, one of the ways I hurt you is that I robbed you of your mom. Little girls should grow up in families being safe and happy and, most important, being able to trust and talk with their moms. Little girls should be able to take their baths and put on pink Strawberry Shortcake pajamas if they want. They should be able to have their moms help them get dressed and, when they need a good night kiss, have their moms carry them into their bedrooms with blue umbrellas on their pink wallpaper. Just before going to bed, little girls should be able to talk with their moms about anything they want. They should be able to trust their moms and ask their moms questions or tell their moms about anything that is bothering them. I remember once when you were little in the market by our house, you asked your mom, "How do the store men get the stems in the apples?" Everyone laughed, but it was a really good question. You wondered about the apple stems and like little girls are supposed to do, you asked your mom.

But then, Susie, I started tricking you and doing secret touching to you. I told you that your mom wouldn't like you any more if you told her what I was doing. I made it seem like you shouldn't talk to your mom or ask your mom any questions. I made you afraid to trust your mom. This was just like robbing a little girl of her mom. This was not fair for me to do because little girls have a right to trust their moms with lots of things. Even though your mom was really wanting to help you, wanting to talk to you, and wanting to answer your questions, I hurt you by making you think you couldn't ask her. I robbed you of your mom by not letting you think you could talk to her about secret touching or apple stems.

After completing his clarification assignments, George wrote a letter to Mary requesting permission to present his clarification to her. George's clarification request letter appears in Table 3.

Table 3
George's Letter Requesting Permission
To Present His Clarification

Dear Mary,

I know that you and I have been talking about sexual abuse for the last year and one- half. In the beginning of this program, I put forth a lot of effort to keep you confused and worried about me. As time has gone on, I have learned to think more about our daughter and to think of your needs. Even though I have talked to you about clarification for many hours, I want to take this opportunity to "officially" ask your permission to talk with you about the crime I have committed.

I don't know what could be worse for a mother than to learn that her husband, her sexual partner, has been sexually offending her very own daughter. Although I will never be able to feel exactly what you feel, I do think I appreciate your position. It must be hard to try to be a good wife and a good mother at the same time.

I would like to ask your permission to meet with you in a therapy session to present my clarification. Even though we have discussed this many times, I wanted to officially ask your permission. The crime I have committed is perhaps worse than death, and I have no right to be Susie's father. For the time being, you are her only parent, and I would like permission to meet with you, to explain my clarification, and give you an opportunity to evaluate whether I should present this clarification to Susie.

Remember, I have been manipulative, intimidating, and controlling in the past. This decision is up to you. I trust you will make the right choice for the benefit of Susie and for your benefit, as well.

Your husband,
George

In accordance with the program guidelines, George first presented Susie's clarification to Mary in her therapist's office. Mary wept quietly and indicated that she had not understood why Susie had not confided in her. She indicated that her feelings for both George and Susie over the past 14 months had ranged from overwhelming guilt to rage. Her reasons for these feelings were because she had no clue as to why Susie seemed to prefer George to her. Mary had avoided regular attendance at the Spouse group, indicating George and Susie had a problem, not her. She understood now that George had managed to convince Susie that Mary was her enemy and would reject Susie if she discovered that "Susie was touching George." Mary exploded with rage at George as she remembered her own abuse and how closely Susie's abuse had paralleled her own. "How could I have not known?"

Although Mary had maintained a passive, almost accepting, exterior to this point, she now expressed doubt about the continuation of the marriage and her ability to ever trust George in the future. George was clearly shaken by Mary's assertiveness and resolve. He started sobbing during one of their joint sessions. Mary turned away and said, "Tears won't get you anything this time, George."

Mary responded to her therapist's encouragement to start working on her own victimization in an Adult Survivor group in order to attempt to resolve that abuse and become more aware of the manipulative patterns of offenders to which many childhood victims respond.

In her therapist's view, the clarification by George to Mary permitted her to stop blaming herself for not being an adequate wife and mother. In addition, it was thought that this clarification got Mary in touch with the fact that she had the right to expect honesty, respect, and equality of treatment in a marriage relationship. Finally, Mary acknowledged that development of her own self-esteem was necessary if she was to help develop the self-esteem of her children.

George and Mary took a few minutes to compose themselves after George had completed his clarification to Mary. George then asked Mary if she would permit him to present his clarification to Susie. Mary's angry reply was, "Why should I permit you to do anything?"

George paused and then replied, "I know that I have lost all rights to ask anything of you or of Susie. But if you have gained some understanding of how I manipulated you and Susie, would it be possible for Susie to also be able to benefit from an explanation of what I did and how I caused her to blame herself and not trust in you?" After a few moments of thought, Mary agreed to let Susie hear George's clarification "if it is Susie's choice and she is prepared and protected by Jan [her therapist]."

Susie agreed to the clarification and began preparation with her therapist and her group for her first contact with her father since his arrest. At first, she was extremely anxious and frightened that George would be angry with her. She decided that she did not want George to see her while he talked to her. Given this situation, the offender-therapist arranged for George to sit in the plethysmography laboratory and speak through a microphone to Susie in the adjoining room. Susie was given the choice of having other people in the room in addition to the victim- and offender-therapist. She decided that she would sit on her therapist's lap and that she did not want anyone else in the room, including her mother.

As George started to present his clarification, Susie became almost rigid and clung tightly to her therapist. However, after George explained how he had tricked Susie into not trusting her mother, Susie asked if her mother could be invited into the room.

Susie sat on her mother's lap for the remainder of that session and several other sessions that followed. She also gave permission for George to come into the same room and seemed to be pleased to see him. She gave him a report on recent school events and accomplishments and George was able to make appropriate responses, although he was on the verge of tears.

In several different ways during the first session Susie asked George "WHY?" he had molested her. She seemed to be testing her own perception of what had been explained by George. Her questions to George included: "Were you really lying about Mom not liking me?" "Why did you tell the police I was lying?" "Why did you want to touch a little kid on her special parts?" "How will I know you won't do it again?"

George told Susie that he was a selfish person who had not considered anyone's feelings but his own. He stated that he knew she wanted other people to be happy and he tricked her by misusing her special quality.

Susie seemed initially satisfied that she did not share any guilt for the abuse. However, in subsequent sessions, she repeatedly asked in different ways if there was something she did to cause the sexual touching.

After the completion of the in-person clarification sessions, George completed a very elaborate scrapbook for Susie. Susie, her mother, siblings, and grandparents contributed very positive letters along with communications from all of the professionals who had been involved in the case since the discovery. Susie was especially affected by the pictures of her that had been taken when the abuse started at age four. Use of the scrapbook in the future was thoroughly explained to Mary: it was intended to be a document of what really happened, how it happened, and a validation of Susie's lack of responsibility for the abuse as well as her worth as an individual. The scrapbook could literally be "put away" and "laid to rest" as a protective "archive for the future" when intrusive memories and perceptions at a later stage of development might require another clarification.

To summarize from the therapists' points of view, George's clarification to his wife and daughter seemed to have a profound effect on repairing and strengthening the mother-daughter relationship as well as in assisting Mary in recognizing that she had some power to control her own life. Susie seemed most relieved that George was not angry at her for telling the truth about what he had done. She was elated to find that her mother really could be trusted. However, it appeared from Susie's general demeanor around males, that her long-term sexualization by George placed her at risk of being vulnerable to future victimization.

Epilogue

The entire family became involved and active in Phase 4, the Aftercare component of the RTAT program. As observed in many sexual offenders, George's long-established pattern of seeking forbidden excitement was eventually manifested in another kind of criminal activity: shortly before the end of his five years of probation, George failed his polygraph, and it was determined that he was stealing from his employer. This resulted in loss of his job, but he found another one at lower pay. The remainder of his probation was uneventful as to criminal behavior.

George and Mary entered marriage counseling. They also attended Act 2 Growth Component classes which centered on parenting and communication skills. Mary eventually decided to divorce George, and for four months the entire family participated in intensive family counseling. This program, sponsored by Child Protective Services, assisted the children, especially Susie, to view the divorce as an adult decision, not a result of the molestation report.

Shortly after the divorce-decision counseling, Susie reported to her mother sexual touching by a friend of the family. The offender was arrested and was found to have molested his own children also. Mary and George were devastated by this discovery. In his aftercare support group George had to deal with the fact that he had probably developed Susie's vulnerability to victimization. It seemed positive, however, that Susie reported the incident immediately and that she chose to report it to her mother.

George appears to have made positive changes in his thinking and has become a competent peer-counselor to newly arrested offenders. Mary eventually left the area with her children and reportedly has remarried.

Summary and Research Recommendations

The results of the above RTAT case study indicate that involving the offender in the payment of emotional restitution through direct therapeutic contact with his victims seemed to: (1) repair some of the damage done to the mother-daughter relationship; (2) improve the mother's sense of power to control her own life; and (3) relieve the victim from guilt and fear instilled by the offender. The fact that the victim in this case study was sexualized to be vulnerable to others by her father and, as a result was later molested by another offender, emphasizes the importance of developing a scrapbook for any future treatment that may be required.

Some preliminary in-house research has already been conducted comparing those offenders who participated in the program without physiological monitoring tools and under the more traditional family therapy approach with offenders who participated in the current treatment format (Hindman, 1989). The results of this research indicate that offenders are not honest about how many individuals they have victimized unless they know their reports will be checked o verified. The average number of victims reported per RTAT offender increased from 1.5 to 9 after the polygraph use started in 1983.[17]

It would be beneficial to conduct outcome studies of relapse among offenders who began treatment under the RTAT model for a minimum of five years after termination of probation. Such research would greatly enhance the validity of this type of victim-oriented treatment.

The most compelling research, however, is not necessarily related to the perpetrator and recidivism but to a greater focus on the rehabilitation of victims. The RTAT model attempts to focus the offender's efforts toward repairing the damage to the victim, believing this process will greatly benefit the perpetrator indirectly. Ideally, the RTAT model can be viewed as a "Victim Treatment Program" with a sex-offender component. Therefore, it seems most appropriate to examine the rehabilitation of the victim, rather than concentrate on the perpetrator's failure or success. Children who have had access to the clarification process and to the resolution scrapbook should be followed for many years to evaluate their recovery and emotional health. The ultimate success of the RTAT program will be measured if victims recognize their innocence, reclaim their childhood, and proceed toward a future of contentment, leaving their victimization behind them as clarified and resolved issues.

---

17. RTAT offenders were compared with respect to self-reported victims at arrest and on their sexual histories. The study also looked at the difference in number of victims reported by RTAT offenders before polygraphs were used and aft.er their use was instituted. See Hindman, J. (1989). Research disputes assumptions about child molesters. *NDAA Bulletin,* 7(4).

Appendix A
PEER-COUNSELING GUIDELINES

1. It is most appropriate when talking to prospective offenders that you introduce yourself as an offender and that you explain to the person that you would like to talk "to them." Emphasize that they do not necessarily have to talk "to you ... about themselves."
2. Put the person at ease by explaining that you know how they are feeling because _ months (years) ago you were in the same situation.
3. Recognize that offenders are typically self-centered people and initially they will respond more to statements about how they can "get help," "feel better," etc. That is not to say that you should not emphasize repairing the damage done to the child but you should make that point by emphasizing the offender's feelings in a statement like, "You will feel so much better if you work toward helping your child."
4. Remember that most offenders will de-emphasize, rationalize, or fabricate information. Don't be too anxious to confront them during the first few times you talk to them. Remember, your goal is to offer support and understanding, to provide information about the RTAT program, and to convince the offender to admit to the charges against him/her.
5. Be prepared for talk about suicide and attempts to flee the area. Focus your talk on helping the offender understand that to stay and face the situation will benefit him/her most effectively.
6. Explain the legal system as best you understand it. Do not make any promises!!! Emphasize that there will be an opportunity to be EVALUATED for entrance to the program. It is only fair that you explain that admitting to the charges or a "guilty" plea does not 100% guarantee entrance to the program. But you can emphasize that cooperation, accepting responsibility for the crime, etc. increases the chances that the person will be accepted. This is also an opportunity for you to explain that you feel the legal system is fair and that you feel the evaluation process is fair and equitable.
7. Explain the program as best you know it. Emphasize honesty, family counseling, fees, groups, etc. It is important to present the program in a way that the offender sees it as something in which he/she can receive help. Usually the offender is not yet tuned in to helping the child but will respond to his/her own benefits.
8. When talking to nonoffending spouses you should emphasize your understanding of their situation by talking about your personal situation. It helps to ask questions about the children's ages, where they were born, how they do in school, etc. Do anything to put the person at ease.
9. Explain the program but be careful in making assumptions about how the spouse feels. Do not, as an example, make a statement that suggests that being in the program automatically indicates that the family will be reunited. Yet do not discount that possibility. The spouse may be feeling very angry about the offender or perhaps very supportive of the offender. Simply explain the program in terms of clarifying and mending everyone's feelings.
10. Do not attack the spouse if she/he is blaming the child. Do not agree with this attitude but simply state that many women initially feel that way but usually change their minds. Do not do excessive confrontation at this point. Offer support and understanding and do everything to have the spouse understand that the program has something for them.
11. Most spouses are concerned with how they contributed to this situation. Try to assist in making them feel that they are not alone and that they can be helped in an effort to make them feel less guilty.
12. Assist the spouse in understanding what the "no-contact" order will mean. Assist her/him in understanding that they must now protect and provide support and comfort for their children. Explain to them how important it is that the offender be separated from the children. Assure them that this is the best way to help themselves, the children, and the offender.
13. It is important that you attempt to have the spouse develop positive feelings about RTAT, CSD [Children's Services Division], and the legal system. Describe how these agencies will be of assistance to her/him, not a threat.
14. Make every attempt to get the spouse, offender, etc., in RTAT as soon as possible. Call RTAT personally if there are conflicts or have a CSD person arrange an appointment.
15. Encourage the spouse or offender to call you or other offenders or spouses if needed.

Appendix B
CLARIFICATION/RESOLUTION ISSUES AND COMPONENTS

The following letter is given to each offender who is a clarification presentation candidate at the Phase 3 point in treatment to serve as a guide in the preparation of both verbal and scrapbook presentations.

Dear Offender:

The word "RESTITUTION" means to pay back or to give back something that you have taken. That is the purpose of this process. In this treatment program, we believe your job is to repair the damage to the victim you have abused. Therefore, this is a very important assignment.

There are many steps toward earning the privilege of working on "clarification. "Before you are able to begin working on this assignment, there are many things you must change and there are many goals that must be completed. Remember, it is a privilege to be working on this portion of the treatment program.

This paper outlines the general components or most typical components of the Resolution/Clarification process. Please remember, EACH VICTIM IS DIFFERENT AND EACH CLARIFICATION MAY HAVE DIF-

FERENT COMPONENTS OR REQUIRE A DIFFERENT PROCESS. This outline is only a general guide to the clarification process.

GREETING:

Due to the emotional level of the victim during the clarification session, the first three minutes after entering the room with your victim are usually so emotionally upsetting that listening is difficult for the victim. Your assignment is to prepare a three- to five-minute Greeting. The Greeting has certain rules and regulations which will be gone over in the group process. The basic goal of the Greeting is to put the victim at ease so continuation in the clarification session will occur. You may not discuss your sexual crime, you may not ask the victim questions, nor are you allowed to discuss "nonsensical" things. You should be able to talk for three minutes, without asking questions, without being powerful and controlling, while creating interest in participating in the remaining portion of the clarification process.

MORNING ASSIGNMENT:

In order to be able to spend time with the victim in a clarification, you must understand how the victim feels on the day of the clarification. Pretend that you are the victim and you have opened your eyes and you have just remembered that today is the day you will be meeting with the person who sexually abused you. From the victim's perspective, write a detailed assignment on how the victim feels the "morning of the clarification."

DESCRIPTION:

The "Description" requires you to describe special things about the victim, but there is a very serious purpose to this process. In your abusive actions, you misused unique qualities in a child in order to keep the secret. Most of these qualities were positive attributes of the child. You must describe eight-to-ten positive qualities in your victim that pertain to your coercion and manipulation. You must be able to describe "childlike" events, actions, or issues that make each point a special unique quality of the victim. And, most important, you must later be able to explain how you used these qualities to ensure the conspiracy.

TRAUMA ASSESSMENT:

You will not be able to prepare a clarification and repair the damage to your victim unless you are aware of how you have hurt the victim. Each victim is damaged in different ways through different things that have happened. Your therapist will be doing a formal Trauma Assessment of your victim in coordination with other professionals in the program. Your therapist will be preparing a typewritten, 8- to 10-page

Trauma Assessment; you are to prepare a Trauma Assessment as well. You must search yourself and discover how your sexual abuse of the victim has caused suffering. The Trauma Assessment should be as long as it would take to convince the victim that you understand something about the damage you have caused. If the Trauma Assessment can be presented in 30 seconds, consider how the victim would feel with that kind of response. A common cry from victims is, "Nobody has any idea how I feel." Through completing this assignment, you will learn something about how the victim feels and how the victim has been hurt.

WHAT HAPPENED:

For this portion of clarification, you are to write a complete description of what actually took place during the sexual abuse. You should begin with the first incident and you should describe the environment, the scene, and the details that will help us understand exactly what occurred. As you write this description, remember that the victim and the victim's family will, more than likely, read this description or hear this description in some form. This description will become part of the victim's clarification book. If what you write is insignificant or lacks details, the victim will obviously assume you are taking the crime lightly. If you write things that are extremely uncomfortable and embarrassing to the victim, you may further traumatize her/him. This assignment must have a delicate balance between explaining what actually happened to avoid secrecy and at the same time protecting the victim from unnecessary trauma.

HOW IT HAPPENED:

This part of your assignment is to describe the secrecy or the coercion that you used to keep the sexual contact private. You are to think about the relationship between yourself and the victim. You are to think about what was happening in the victim's life and you are to think about any other things that allowed you to involve the child in a conspiracy. In other words, you are to describe for the victim and the victim's family how you were able to abuse this child without the child telling or stopping the abuse. Each part of the Description must be discussed in this portion of the clarification. You may, however, go beyond the points mentioned in the Description if you choose. From this assignment, the victim must have a perfect understanding of how you were able to accomplish the abuse, and the victim must be protected from all guilt and blame for failing to stop the abuse.

WHY THIS HAPPENED:

You are required to describe in detail why you abused this victim. Remember, this explanation will be read by the parents of the victim, as well. Whatever reason you give for committing your crime will, more than likely, have an impact on the victim's life forever. You must write a clear, crisp explanation of why you sexually abused *this* child and why you are responsible for the damage. You must make sure the victim understands not only about you, but about sexuality in general so this portion of the clarification is clear. There should be no doubt in the victim's mind after this portion of the clarification that you were solely responsible for what took place. There should also be no doubt that future sexual decisions for the victim are not connected to your crime.

TROUBLE SHOOTING: (verbal presentation only)

Before you will be allowed to participate in the clarification, your therapist must have a sense that you are competent to deal with any emergencies that should arise. Usually, these emergencies happen during the first few minutes of the clarification. In group therapy, you must demonstrate your confidence in knowing how to deal with these things:
1. What to do if the child starts crying.
2. What to do if the child jumps up and hits you.
3. What to do if the child apologizes for telling.
4. What to do if the child says, "I love you."
5. What to do if the child jumps up and tries to show you affection without saying anything.
   These are just a few examples of the kinds of things that can happen in a clarification. You must show your therapist that you know how to deal with each one of these issues before you can participate in a clarification.

LETTERS OF PERMISSION:
You are required to write letters of permission to the victim, to the victim's parents, and to anyone else who may be asked to participate in a clarification. These letters must request permission to meet with these individuals. Remember, *the victim and the victim's family have total power and control regarding whether or not they wish to cooperate with the clarification process.* Letters to the guardians of the victim should simply be "to ask permission for a clarification." The victim's parents may then decide after meeting with you personally whether they will allow you to proceed. Remember, all of your rights have been taken away because of the crime you have committed. Regardless of how hard you have worked on preparing for the clarification, you are not in control and the victim or the victim's family has the right to refuse.

Remember, the work that you are putting together will be placed in a scrapbook for the victim and family. These documents will become part of the victim's file, and in many cases, will be given to the victim to keep forever. The final steps in completing the scrapbook will be explained to you at a much later time, but from this paper, you should understand the steps toward preparing for a clarification.

Appendix C
ACT 2 GROUPS AND CLASSES

MANDATED COMPONENTS FOR OFFENDERS

The following classes are required for Act 2 offenders and are offered sequentially on a quarterly basis as money for instructors is available. Spouses are encouraged to attend these growth component classes. The information is designed to assist those clients with reunification decisions, to strengthen the family unit, and to enhance self-esteem.

Human Sexuality: teen-agers are also encouraged to join parents in attending this class.

Effective Parenting: raising emotionally healthy children, positive discipline, etc.

Effective Interpersonal Communication: saying what you mean, listening skills, etc.

Personal Development: including anger management, job seeking skills, resume writing, grooming, wardrobe planning, color analysis, and makeup.

NONMANDATEDSUPPORTGROUPS

The following are offered on a quarterly basis:

Crisis-Orientation-Support: the program coordinator and several Act 2 peer-counselors administer information to new offenders and family members. This component provides a place for individuals in crisis, generally adult survivors who need assistance while they wait for admittance to the adult survivor group. This is the setting in which the offender contract is presented and explained to those individuals who are requesting admission to the program.

Act 2 Offenders: sometimes divided to enable adult survivors to deal with their own victimization.

Couples: offered only as needed because many couple issues are addressed in growth component classes.

Act 2 Teens: for both male and female "graduates" of primary treatment. RTAT also accepts some graduates of local substance abuse programs who need ongoing support from peers.

Act 2 Preteens: for both male and female "graduates" between ages 9 and 12.

Self-esteem for Kids: structured play for children while parents attend the Act 2 activities; this serves as an excellent monitoring vehicle for children in newly reunited families.

Spanish Speakers: includes Act 2 Spanish speaking offenders and both primary and Aftercare spouses and adult victims who are unable.to benefit from participation in an English speaking group. This requires an incredibly skilled and flexible leader.

Adult Women Molested as Children: the only exclusive primary treatment group that meets at the Act 2 evening time (to assist those women who need childcare).

OTHER ACT 2 ACTIVITIES

Peer-Counselors (See Appendix A): Act 2 offenders and other family members are encouraged to consider becoming peer-counselors. Training is offered in both a formal class and informally "on the job." Individuals are encouraged to assist in the Crisis-Orientation-Support group to observe group process, interviewing, and helping techniques.

An Act 2 Crisis-Support coordinator accepts referrals from interagency professionals and assigns specific peer-counselors to contact members of new families. One couple is still very active after 9 years, and about 10 nonmandated offenders continue to participate voluntarily in the program.

Leadership Opportunities: Act 2 has bylaws, committees and officers similar to other service organizations. Officers meet on a monthly basis to plan the business agenda, and a monthly business meeting is held for the entire membership. Officers include a president, vice president (in charge of ways and means), secretary, crisis-support coordinator, and a voting representative to the RTAT Board of Directors. The RTAT business manager serves as treasurer.

Each offender still on probation is required to make restitution to the community by serving on one major committee which supports the treatment program. This has included a variety of fund-raising activities over the years (raffles, bazaars, car washes, and donkey baseball). At the present time, Act 2 sponsors community Bingo games twice a month which cover much of RTAT's overhead expense. Recently, Act 2 offenders donated 1,000 hours of labor to complete a major remodeling project for the program.

Each year, the Act 2 group sponsors an Award Night which recognizes all the program volunteers, the graduates of the children's groups, and the professionals. The program is always a time of inspiration and renewal for the interagency team members, especially the police and investigators who would otherwise experience only the agony and trauma at discovery.

The RTAT program coordinator serves as an advisor to the Act 2 government. However, the membership decides on projects, activities, and the methods used to accomplish them. For many individuals, Act 2 is their first experience with recognition for committee participation and leadership.

Chapter 3
THE SYSTEMIC/ATTRIBUTIONAL MODEL: VICTIM-SENSITIVE OFFENDER THERAPY[1]

Walter H. Bera[2]

Abstract

In this treatment approach, survivor-offender communications are based on understanding interpersonal violence within a systemic/ attributional model. The treatment program emphasizes victim safety, rights, and empowerment during offender treatment in a parallel process. In this program the offender's therapist maintains a victim- sensitive position within the offender's treatment milieu. The therapist offers information disclosed by the offender to help the victim's recovery, and whenever possible, modifies the offender's behavior contracts based on ongoing input from the victim. Victims and their families ultimately may choose among a range of closure options involving survivor-offender communication interventions. This program model recognizes the larger social context of the abuse.

Introduction and Treatment Philosophy

This chapter presents a new paradigm for understanding interpersonal violence: the systemic and attributional model. A "systemic" and "attributional" critique of society's current response to sexual abuse is presented and a Victim-Sensitive Offender Therapy (V- SOT) model is proposed as an essential part of comprehensive treatment for both victims and offenders. A system perspective emphasizes the whole of a problem rather than its parts (Bateson, 1972). It emphasizes the contextual and interactional dynamic of abuse-the behaviors of the offender-victim dyad. This "system view" points out that while the vast majority of sexual abuse occurs most frequently within intimate family and social systems (i.e., between family members, relatives, friends, or acquaintances), victims and offenders are generally treated in a fragmented, inadequate, and isolated manner, ignoring the *context* in which the abuse occurred. Furthermore, since both victims and offenders verbalize and act on misattributions of responsibility, they can be most completely treated by bringing victims and offenders together in a carefully prepared, safe, and controlled context.

This coordinated model is not the entirety of sex-offender treatment, but one part of the process. Offender-victim interactions *potentially* have the most positive impact on victims of any contact with the legal or social service systems involved in abuse reports. But if such interactions are not utilized or if they are done primarily for the offender's benefit, they can have a profoundly negative impact on victims. The primary goal of victim-sensitive offender- victim interactions is to empower victims while protecting their safety. The secondary goal is to enhance the offender's sense of responsibility for his/her actions while increasing the offender's awareness of their true impact.

---

1 It has been a struggle to develop an appropriate title to capture the essence of the model. One suggested title among many was "Survivor-offender Mediation Process".
2 Special thanks to Fay Honey Knopp who supported the development of this paper as first presented at the Task Force on Restorative Justice retreat in Guelph, Ontario in October, 1986. Continued work has been supported in part by a grant from the Hubert H. Humphrey Institute Conflict and Change Center.

In victim-sensitive offender therapy, the treatment provider can carve out a role of being the *victim's* advocate within the *offender's* social service, legal, psychiatric, and family milieu. That role involves using those offender-oriented systems to address the victim's concerns about the offender's past, present, and future abusive behavior. The sex-offender treatment provider tells the offender up front, "I'm *your* therapist, but I am also the victim's advocate." Being the victim's advocate enables the offender's therapist to call him to account for what he's done.

In general, offenders and victims may get similar three-stage treatment: (1) their treatment needs are assessed; (2) individual and/or group therapy works toward confronting and correcting the clients' misattributions of responsibility (victim's self-blame or guilt; offender's victim- or system-blame); and (3) clients write letters reflecting their new attributions and resulting feelings (confrontation letters by victims, apology letters by offenders). The letters in most cases are not sent. The difference in this model is that the aborted interaction is fulfilled. If the victim permits, the offender sends a letter of apology. If the victim and/or the parents choose to participate, real-life meetings with the offender are held, enabling a real-rather than symbolic-closure on the abuse experience.

Further research on outcomes is needed-sensitively designed longitudinal studies-for both victims and offenders who participate in restorative offender-victim inter- actions.

Although this study is on juvenile sex offenders, the model has also been used with adult sex offenders and with juvenile and adult sexual abuse *victims.* The treatment stages are significantly longer for adult offenders than for juveniles. This three-stage model can be applied to the task of organizing the multiple issues in sexual abuse cases in general.

Critique of Current Methods
Sexual Abuse Occurs within the Victim's Family or Social System
The majority of victims of sexual assault are abused by someone they know and should be able to trust: a family member, relative, neighbor, or acquaintance. Between 50 and 80 percent of all child victims were sexually abused by people known to them. Parents, step-parents, or relatives were responsible for 30-to-50 percent of all cases, with neighbors, babysitters, or friends involved in most of the remainder (Finkelhor, 1984; Peters, Meyer, & Carroll, 1976; Sgroi, 1975). In these studies, over one-third of the assaults occurred in the child's home, while 20 percent occurred in the home of the offender. Adolescents and adult victims were more likely to encounter physical force or violence, usually in acquaintance or marital rape situations (Keller, 1980).

The therapist-client relationship, which demands a high level of intimacy and trust and entails special vulnerability on the part of the client, is responsible for a significant amount of sexual abuse. In anonymous surveys, 10-to-15 percent of mental health professionals admit engaging in sexual contact with their clients; the actual percentage is considered much higher (Schoener, Milgrom, Gonsiorek, Luepker, & Conroe, 1989).

All of these studies demonstrate that incidents of forced, tricked, or manipulated sexual touch are usually committed by people who *use* their intimacy with the victim to perpetrate their abusive behavior; such incidents represent a fundamental breach of trust in society's most basic and precious relationships. Such crimes of intimacy shake the victim's basic "faith in the world" and understandably lead to the well-documented sequels of abuse: victim guilt, shame, phobia, fear of again risking intimacy, nightmares, developmental disturbance, etc. (Briere, 1984; Burgess & Holmstrom, 1975; Finkelhor, 1984; Keller, 1980; Peters et al., 1976).

Traditional Treatment is Fragmented, Inadequate and Isolated

The treatment perspective traditionally adopted by professionals working with either victims or offenders focuses on the individual's personality or family background, thereby ascribing etiology and treatment strategies to individual psychological dynamics. Classical criminology suggests that the offender's personality develops from his socio-cultural conditions; such a view ascribes the offender's criminal behavior to those conditions (Sutherland & Cressey, 1978). Both paradigms divide the sexual abuse event into at least two parts-victim *or* offender-and logically lead to the kind of fragmented responses critiqued here.

Social service and criminal justice systems often respond to sex crimes in an inadequate, fragmented, and piecemeal fashion. Typically, reports of child abuse are investigated by county child protection workers with the help of the police. If the offender is a family member (i.e., father), the child is often removed from the home in a traumatic and frequently revictimizing experience. Recognizing this dilemma, more enlightened counties remove the offender to provide the child with the necessary degree of protection.

In cases where the victims are adults, the police investigate the abuse, while support may be provided by victim assistance programs or rape crisis center workers, where such programs are available.

Both child and adult victim cases are usually referred to the courts where restraining orders and confidentiality laws (intended to protect the victim), and attorney's strategic advice (intended to protect the "alleged" offender's rights) may further alienate the participants and exacerbate their trauma.

"No-talk" rules embodied in these legal devices increase the misattribution of responsibility: the victim assumes blame for the abuse and its consequences (often based on direct or indirect messages from the offender and/or other family members), while the offender (often aided by his lawyer) projects all blame onto the victim and paints himself as the innocent victim of circumstance, of a misunderstanding, and/or of the system. Thus, the adversarial legal process tends to cement counter-therapeutic mindsets in victims and offenders. The full dimension of these attributional processes will be commented on later in this chapter.

While offenders may be ordered by the courts into treatment and may receive coordinated state- or county-funded services, a significant proportion of sexual abuse *victims* receive no treatment for their abuse-related trauma. Officials often pay inadequate attention to their concerns. In cases where children are victims of extended family members or neighbors, the only help offered may be a pamphlet handed out after the evidentiary interview. Although psychotherapy might help, often it is unavailable or too expensive. Many parents do not pursue professional help because of their embittering experience with the system and conflicted loyalties to the identified offender. Child sexual abuse forms the largest category of all reported sex crimes, yet of the offenders with whom this writer has worked, only a minority of their victims had any contact with a professional therapist.

While adult victims *may* receive help from the network of rape crisis centers (avail- able primarily in urban settings), the victim must actively search out the services and maintain therapy contact for complete treatment. For a number of reasons, however, including an inability to offer victims what is most needed, rape crisis centers often fail to provide adequate support for victims to complete treatment; in most cases they have redefined their mission in terms of crisis management and advocacy rather than treatment.

After the abuse report, and *if* there is a confession or legally "sufficient" evidence, sex offenders can be placed in a criminal "correctional" facility, residential treatment facility, or simply court-ordered into outpatient treatment as a condition of probation. Often some combination of the above is recommended. Prison and residential treatment facilities usually treat the offender in isolation from the community with an individual and group therapy format. Even in incest cases there is often no sensitive opportunity for the victim to express her/his issues vis-a-vis the offender: no forum is offered for the victim to develop a therapeutic sense of power. Often, the next time the victim hears about the offender after the initial investigation or trial is an announcement of the offender's impending release. "Untreated" victims commonly contact rape crisis centers or mental health clinics for help at this time.

Generally, victims and offenders are treated together in outpatient programs *only* if both are members of an intact nuclear family. If there has been a divorce or the victims are outside the immediate family, attempts at achieving a therapeutic resolution of the abuse events between the victim and offender are rarely made.

In extrafamilial pedophilia and rape, the victim is not considered a part of treatment, and no attempts are made to confront the issues between the two people most involved.

In contrast to current fragmented, isolated treatment modes, Gulotta and deCataldo-Neuberger (1983) argue for a very different, holistic perspective. They argue for a systemic and attributional approach to the whole field of criminology and victimology:

> It should be no longer concentrated only on the victim's (or offender's) personality and on his socio-cultural condition, but should embrace the dyad, criminal-victim, a system which cannot be separated without inciting the same criticism aimed at all psychological currents of individualistic trend (p. 5).

Attribution Issues
Offender Misattributions: Blaming Victims, Excusing Themselves
Attribution theory was developed within the field of social psychology and offers a useful perspective on sexual abuse. As Kelley and Thibaut (1969) have defined it, "Attribution theory describes the process by which the individual seeks and attains conceptions of the stable dispositions or attributes" (p. 5). An action, such as sexual abuse, can be attributed to causes in the en-

vironment or in the situation, or to the underlying dispositions of the persons involved. The mainstay of the attributional process is that "intent" is imputed rather than observed. Heider (1958) was the first to call the attention of psychologists to the fact that actions are controlled more by how an event is *perceived* than by what actually happens.

Offender misattributions have been well documented in the literature. Scully and Marolla (1984) interviewed 114 convicted male rapists to examine the motivations and attributions they used to explain their behavior. The article (aptly titled "Convicted Rapists' Vocabulary of Motive: Excuses and Justifications") reported that these convicted rapists' attributions of blame or minimization to the victim fell into five major categories: (1) women are seductresses; (2) women mean "yes" and say "no"; (3) most women eventually relax and enjoy it; (4) nice girls don't get raped; and (5) the sexual assault was only a minor wrongdoing.

Similar attributions of fault to the victim are also found in various analog studies using male and female college undergraduates (Shotland & Goodstein, 1983) and medical students (Gilmartin, 1983). A possible explanation for the similarity of attribution to the victim by diverse subject pools was posited by Lerner (1980). He theorized that people are inclined to believe in a "just world," a place where individuals "get what they deserve and deserve what they get." According to this belief, the criterion of "deserving" is the quality of "goodness" or "evilness" attributed to the personality or the behavior that brings about the good or the evil result. In order to maintain their view of the world as "just," people need such attributions of fault-or negative disposition-to victims. If bad things can happen to good people, the same could happen to them. The "just world" view thus becomes a "defensive attribution."

Study subjects also attribute fault to sexual abuse victims regardless of age. Using scenarios involving child and adolescent victims with an adult offender, Waterman and Foss- Goodman (1984) replicated many of the adult and peer assault victim-blaming results. Regardless of the victim's age (7, 11, or 15 years old) and the offender's adult status, respondents placed some responsibility for the sexual abuse on the victim. The major reason respondents gave for blaming child victims was, "The victims should have resisted." Significantly, subjects also blamed the nonparticipating parents of the victims because they "should have protected the victim" or in some way contributed to the victimizing event.

Results indicate that both subject characteristics and victim characteristics relate to how much victims are blamed.[3] Respondents whose answers exhibited sexual conservatism and acceptance of interpersonal violence were more likely to find fault with the victim's behavior. Subjects who reported histories as victims of molestation blamed victims less than subjects who did not report such past incidents. Waterman and Foss-Goodman (1984) have further suggested that "blaming the victims may contribute to a climate conducive to child- molesting." A better understanding of the determinants of victim-blaming may lead to strategies for changing these attitudes. Scully and Marolla's (1984) findings also included rapists who admitted responsibility for their

---

3. Participants completed a sexual-attitude questionnaire and personal history. They then read various sexual abuse scenarios and completed an attribution questionnaire after each one.

behavior. These men had developed excuses permitting them to view their behavior as idiosyncratic rather than typical; therefore, they believed that they were not *really* rapists. Their attributions to themselves sort into three main categories: (1) they were under the influence of alcohol or drugs and thereby had diminished responsibility for the rape; (2) their act was a result of emotional problems that diminished their responsibility; and (3) they painted an image of themselves as "nice guys" in an attempt to minimize the crime and negotiate a non-rapist identity. Admitters projected the image of someone who had made a serious mistake, but who in every other respect was a decent person. Their severe minimization of the effects of the abuse and their responsibility for them was readily apparent. Scully and Marolla noted that this lack of personal acceptance of responsibility is fertile ground for the development of future sexual misconduct.

In Waterman and Foss-Goodman (1984), respondents attributed blame to the *adult offender* in child sexual abuse scenes for the following reasons (in descending frequency of report): (1) the offender. abused power; (2) the offender was "sick"; (3) the offender was morally wrong; (4) adults should know better; and (5) the offender must have ignored the child's protests.

In the same study, respondents attributed fault to the *nonparticipating mother and father of the victim* because: (1) the parents should not have left the child alone; (2) the parents should have taught the child how to prevent abuse; and (3) the parents did not elicit the child's ability to confide in them.

Furthermore, when the offender is the *spouse* of the parent, the *non-abusive parent* (usually the mother) was faulted for: (1) not sexually satisfying the offending spouse; (2) not having taught the child how to prevent abuse; and (3) not being the kind of parent in whom the child could confide.

Misattributions by Victims: Guilt and Self-Blame

Numerous studies (Burgess & Holmstrom, 1975; Landis, 1956; Peterson, 1976) found that child victims of sexual abuse tended to keep the secret from their parents because they felt it was in some way their own fault and they feared rejection, blame, punishment, or abandonment for this confusing and often terrifying event. The personal and psychological effects on the victim and family can be multiple: fear of safety at home, eating and/or sleeping disturbances, nightmares, learning disorders, as well as numerous other trauma that are now suggested as constituting a "post-sexual abuse trauma syndrome" (Briere, 1984).

Because of the many attributional dynamics and their serious consequences, therapists who work with sexual abuse victims emphasize that the sexual abuse is *never* the victim's fault, that it is serious, and that victims may experience it as life-threatening. Becoming angry about the abuse and going through a grieving process are therapeutic for the victim in "letting go" of ruminating on the abuse events. Developing a sense of self-control and mastery over their own life situations is enhanced by such techniques as assertiveness training and self-defense classes (Bera, 1980).

These misattribution-laden mindsets on the part of both victims and offenders warrant coordinated assessment and treatment planning that would benefit the involved clients, families, and professionals. Unfortunately, few current treatment approaches pro- vide such a holistic approach; most therefore fail to offer any therapeutic closure options for those most involved and affected by the abuse events: the victim and offender.

Systemic Perspectives for Survivor-offender Issues

A systemic and contextually based process involving controlled interaction between victim and offender is a common therapeutic strategy in incest treatment (Goodwin, 1982). This process is coordinated by the family therapist and provides critical information and therapeutic experiences for completing treatment in a systematic way. This process empowers the victims with additional information, a sense of safety and respect, and finally, new choices that can lead to a more satisfying and complete resolution of the abuse.

Gelinas (1988, p. 25) emphasizes that individual and group therapy for trauma work "is necessary but not sufficient to resolve the negative effects of incest on the victim's life. It is also therapeutically essential to work with the particular relational issues sur- rounding incestuous child sexual abuse." Working through these issues is done through face- to-face family therapy that includes both the offender and the victim.

Another example of a systemic approach aimed at increasing appropriate avenues for therapeutic closure is the Survivor-offender Reconciliation Programs (VORP) that have existed for a number of years (Knopp, et al., 1976; Umbreit, 1985; Wright & Galaway, 1989). These programs bring victims and offenders together in a controlled, safe and supervised process and have been used successfully in robbery, assault, vandalism, and other crimes (Green, 1984). A body of literature and a number of professional associations have developed within the VORP movement.[4]

Concerns regarding the VORP approach *focus* on the inappropriateness of using a "reconciliation" or "mediation" model in crimes of interpersonal violence because of the significant power disparity between offender and victim. "Mediation" and "reconciliation" imply that two sides "compromise" and agree on some "middle ground." The movement has recognized that such language is clearly inappropriate in cases of sexual abuse or physical violence.

This process is more accurately portrayed in new language and conceptual frames (most clearly developed by Zehr, 1990) as seeking "restorative justice" when injustice has occurred. Sexual and physical abuse are abuses of power and authority, most often from an offender's position of trust, over a vulnerable and available victim. The aim is to empower the victim and restore justice by having the offender take responsibility for the offense and offer appropriate contrition, restitution, and apologies in a personal and meaningful way (for a detailed history and discussions of these issues with illustrative cases see Wright and Galaway, 1989).

---

4. Important VORP organizations include the U.S. Association for Victim/Offender Mediation in Valpariso, Indiana, (219) 462-1127, and Network: Interaction for Conflict Resolution in Kitchener, Ontario in Canada (519) 744-6739.

The systemic model outlined in this chapter attempts in both conceptualization and language to be "victim sensitive." Ethically, it values the safety, rights, and needs of the victim as primary.

In workshops on the model, the traditional training of therapists and social workers is challenged because the issues move outside the boundaries of discrete "disciplines" and press for a holistic or systemic view. Such a view helps overcome the dilemmas that their disciplines (as normally defined) force them into, while safely attempting a more complete therapeutic resolution of interpersonal violence. A summary of the systems perspectives involved in a sexual abuse case appears in Figure 1.

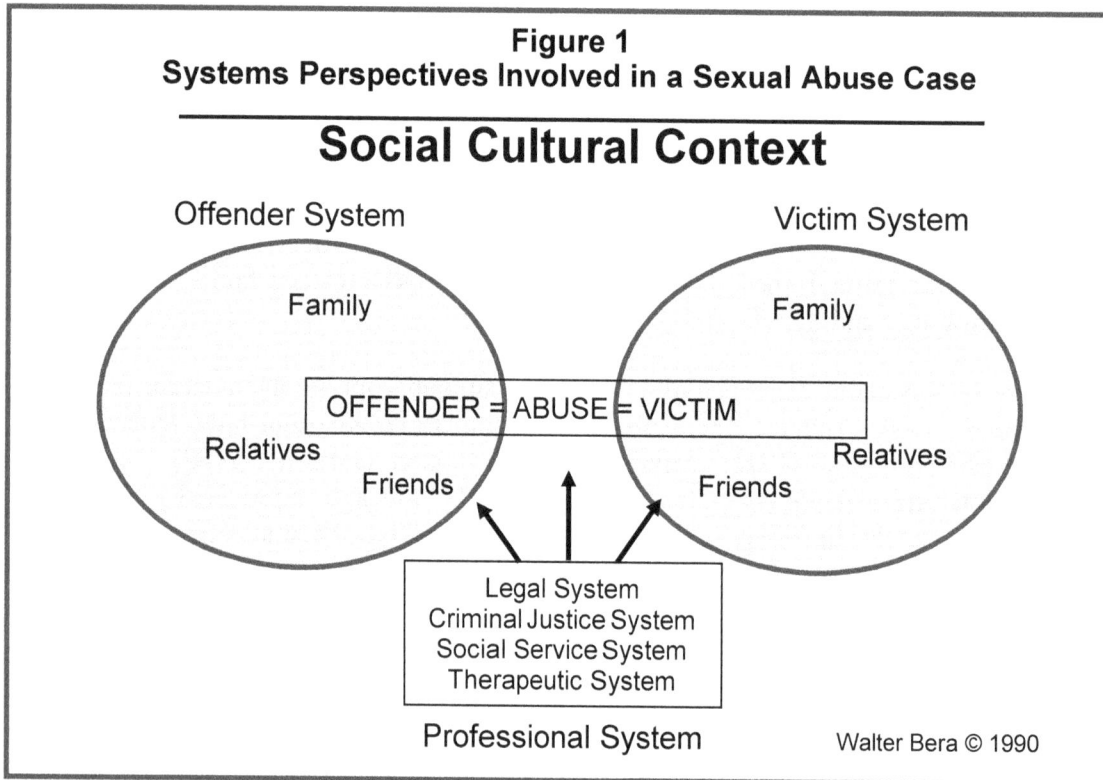

Figure 1
Systems Perspectives Involved in a Sexual Abuse Case

Social Cultural Context

Offender System

Victim System

Family

Family

OFFENDER = ABUSE = VICTIM

Relatives

Relatives

Friends

Friends

Legal System
Criminal Justice System
Social Service System
Therapeutic System

Professional System

Walter Bera © 1990

Treatment Description

Victim-Sensitive Offender Therapy (V-SOT) was designed to overcome the afore- mentioned systemic dilemmas while redefining the VORP or mediation model from a victim- sensitive ethical, safety, and rights position more appropriate for sexual offense treatment.

To use this model, therapists working with sex offenders need to see the rights, feelings, and safety of the victim(s) (or potential victims) of their clients' behavior as their primary concern; at the same time, they must avoid jeopardizing the rights of the offender in the process. This ethical stance should guide every view, insight, and decision the therapist makes regarding the offender.[5]

---

5. For an excellent review of the ethical issues in psychological interventions with clients involved in the criminal justice system, see Monahan (1980).

While this position runs counter to traditional "client-centered" training, it is a logical consequence of a systemic, ethical, and attributional analysis of sexual abuse and has the following strengths:

- It keeps the offender fully responsible for his abusive behavior.
- It minimizes misattribution of fault to the victim.
- The therapist is prevented from inadvertently colluding with the offender against the victim.
- It keeps the offender "out of trouble" by early on confronting any malicious gossip and indirect "get-backs" directed against the victim or family.
- The therapist maintains a clear ethical perspective throughout treatment, minimizing confusion at decision points.
- It maintains a survivor-offender system view throughout that can maximize the degree of therapeutic closure for both victim and offender.
- It helps ensure completeness of treatment for the offender and thereby minimizes the potential for victimizing behavior.
- It gives the therapist more complete information at each stage to make sound treatment plans by supplementing traditional reliance on the offender's self- report with ongoing victim input;
- The therapist is able to maintain a high level of credibility with other involved professionals (e.g. judge, child protection worker, social worker, probation/parole supervisor, etc.) by keeping the victim's interest at heart and soliciting the input of all concerned.

The three-stage V-SOT process was developed while the author was working at the Program for Healthy Adolescent Sexual Expression (PHASE), the largest outpatient, family- based, adolescent sex-offender treatment program in Minnesota. It is the source of significant theory and research on the juvenile offender (Bera, 1985; Mathews, Matthews, & Speltz, 1989; O'Brien & Bera, 1986; O'Brien, 1989). A brief description of the V-SOT process follows; it does not include a description of concurrent clinical treatment of the offender's sexually abusive behavioral pattern.

Ideally, this therapeutic process should be undertaken only after the offender has pled guilty and no lawsuits are contemplated by the involved parties. If either the victim or the offender has unusual life events or stresses, V-SOT should be delayed to a more appropriate time. The clinician clarifies that there is no way to predict or guarantee the participants' behavior and fosters reasonable expectations. Both victim and offender have the right to stop at any point of the process. Clinical judgment and the particularities of each case should guide the application of this or any resolution model.

Stage 1: Communication Switchboard

This stage sets the context and expectations for the assessment and V-SOT process. At intake, or shortly after the juvenile sex offender begins the assessment process, the V-SOT therapist assumes a central role as communication coordinator, or "switchboard," among all concerned participants, including the probation officer, previous therapists, the offender, and the victim (or parents for victims who are underage). The clinician explains the V-SOT model, its stages, goals, and why certain information must be shared with other treatment personnel agencies, and the victim, her/his family, and their therapist. The offender (or parents/ guardian) then signs release forms allowing the therapist to get the offender's police statements and to contact the victim(s) (or parents/guardian). This is the point at which the therapist says to the client, "I'm your therapist, but I am also the victim's advocate."

The communication switchboard stage allows the offender's therapist to do a more complete and contextually sensitive assessment of his/her client by getting all sides of the sexual abuse experience. Only a small minority of teenage sex offenders are completely honest about their sexual abuse or fully recognize the effects of the abuse on their victim(s), but they often are open to their therapist contacting the victim in hopes of making therapeutic progress and increasing the potential for achieving closure.

The offender's therapist calls the victim(s) (or parents/guardian) to let them know the disposition of the case (i.e., "Frank pled guilty and is now on probation; he's in our outpatient treatment program"). It is not unusual for quite a bit of time to have passed since the abuse report, and victims may be left wondering what the results were of the investigatory or legal process. This telephone call is often the first concrete information they have received about the offender since the investigation or trial.

In this phone call, the therapist supports the victim or parents for reporting the abuse, despite any frustrating or traumatizing interactions they may have had with the social service and/or legal systems. Only about a quarter of the victims or their concerned persons contacted have been involved in any kind of therapy. Often, they are embittered by the investigatory and legal process they have gone through, and do not trust asking for further "professional" help. During the intervening time since the investigation, however, new thoughts or concerns may have come to mind that they may wish to share with a therapist. The V-SOT therapist educates parents to the need for victim treatment, where and from whom they can get it, and how it can be funded (victim-assistance programs, victim's compensation, and/or restitution provisions in the offender's sentence). The V-SOT therapist solicits any concerns the victim and/or parents have about the abuse, the victim's trauma- based behavior changes, or about continued emotionally intrusive behavior by the offender. The therapist helps the parents sort out their primary concern (helping the victim to heal) from their feelings of loss of relationship to the offender or the offender's family.

Since the offender is usually a neighbor or family member, some level of emotion- ally intrusive behavior may be continuing: the babysitter-offender rides his bike past the victim's house every day; the two families encounter each other every Sunday at nine o'clock mass; gossip employing sexual innuendo and targeting the victim as "promiscuous" or "queer" haunts the victim at school. The V-SOT treatment provider justifies the victim's trust and confidence in him/her by "fixing it" whenever possible through alterations in the offender's behavior contract or amplified interpretations of existing court orders. The V-SOT therapist encourages the victim to ask any questions about the abuse she/he would like the offender to answer and to continue reporting any inappropriate offender behavior. By talking with the offender's therapist and seeing concrete results, the victim may develop a sense of power and straight-forward control of her/his situation. Ideally the victim feels that what she/he went through then-and is currently experiencing-is important and is finally being heard.

The input of the victim and/or parents has direct impact on the offender's treatment by: (1) providing corroborating or contradictory evidence regarding the offender's disclosure of offense behaviors; and (2) by exposing the offender's subsequent intimidation or power/ control behaviors.

After explaining that the information will be used to confirm or confront information in the offender's disclosure, the V-SOT therapist asks the victim or parents/guardian to sign releases of information for copies of the victim's police statement and interview with the Child Protection Services worker. If the victim is in therapy, the family will be asked to give permission for the victim's therapist to consult with the V-SOT therapist.

In this initial stage, the V-SOT therapist begins to enlist the victim(s) and their concerned persons in an ongoing information-sharing and therapy process. They learn that they will be provided with information, options, and choices as needed, and that the V-SOT therapist is a significant supportive contact within the offender's milieu who will be at their service in the months to come.

Stage 2: Confront Misattributions and Check Progress

Stage 2 for adolescent offenders occurs three to four months into the treatment program. The offender must complete a verbal or written "abuse biography," detailing his history of abusive sexual behavior. The V-SOT therapist checks this document for misattributions the offender continues to hold against the victim and determines whether: (1) the offender fully accepts blame/responsibility for deciding to engage in his abusive behavior; (2) the offender clearly knows the effects of the abuse on the victim; and (3) the offender accepts full responsibility for the consequences of his behavior to himself (in other words, he does not blame the victim or "the system" for where he is now). All three conditions must be met before going on to Stage 3.

After the offender completes his "abuse biography," he writes a "letter of apology" to the victim and victim's parents in order to begin making amends for his crime. The offender reads his biography and letter in his individual, group, and family therapy sessions. The offender's therapist, family, and/or treatment group may reject the documents; the offender rewrites and/or rereads them until they are accepted as both convincing and sincere. Sincerity in the abuse biography or the letter is assessed by looking at omissions of fact or feeling, victim-blaming language, or incongruent affect while the offender is reading. Any inappropriate content or incongruent affect is confronted with feedback from therapist, family, and group ("If your victim were here listening to this, I don't think she'd believe you").

Writing the letter (often only one or two paragraphs) is usually more stressful for adolescent offenders than writing several pages of abuse biography-perhaps because it is a more personal and direct admission of responsibility.

If the victim is in therapy and has given permission, the V-SOT therapist consults with the victim's therapist to check on the progress the victim has made. The consultation provides two-way "reality checking": for the V-SOT therapist to compare the effects of the abuse and the victim's memory of events with the offender's self-reported abuse biography; and for the victim's therapist (or parents/guardian) to have access to the offender's abuse biography and police statements as a reality-check for the victim (especially valuable when the victim dissociated during the abuse). New information from the offender may help explain victim behaviors or phobias that were not thought to be abuse-related.

The offender should not be allowed contact with the victim until his biography and letters are approved, he shows no tendency to blame the victim, and the victim does not blame her/himself.

Finally, the V-SOT therapist provides a progress report on the offender's readiness to continue the process, offers other information that may be useful, and again solicits any questions the victim may have regarding the abuse.

Stage 2 has three major goals: **(1)** to confront any continued sexual abuse misattributions; (2) to complete a progress assessment of the offender and the victim; and (3) to revise the offender's treatment plan and treatment expectations in preparation for Stage 3.

These goals are important in developing plans and expectations for the level of closure the victim chooses in Stage 3. Offenders and victims and their families may have high hopes that the closure session will "fix" everything, so that their lives can go back to "normal." The clinician clearly outlines what can be accomplished in each level of closure in order to prevent the victim or the offender from being disappointed or having a sense of failure. The V-SOT therapist helps the victim and her/his family plan what to expect so they do not feel "used" in the process, while not opening the offender to an inappropriate blast of anger (a potential effect of unresolved issues left over from unrelated abuse episodes previously experienced by the victim *or* by the victim's parents) that could be counter-therapeutic.

Stage 3: Closure Choices

Stage 3 may occur when the adolescent sex offender has been in treatment for 5 to 12-plus months. It is the last major task in the offender's V-SOT process. The offender is nearing completion of his other treatment components; his abuse biography and letters of apology have been accepted by his therapist, family, and peer treatment group; he accepts full responsibility for all aspects of his abusive behavior; and he has some understanding of the effects of his behavior on his victim.

The V-SOT therapist contacts the victim (or her/his therapist and parents) to discuss the closure process. The V-SOT therapist outlines three levels of closure and gives the victim time to decide which one she/he will choose:

1. The offender will continue to comply with the "no-contact" contract into the future. The V-SOT therapist makes a commitment on behalf of the offender that the contract will be followed, backing up that commitment with a promise that he/she will relay any breaches of the contract to the offender's probation officer.
2. The offender 11 mail a letter of apology to the victim. The V-SOT therapist offers (with the offender's informed consent) whatever closing information about the offender's process that the victim asks for or that might be helpful to her/him.

3. The offender (and his family, if appropriate) will attend a face-to-face meeting in a setting the victim chooses for her/his comfort, with any support people she/he chooses. At the meeting, the offender will read his apology letter(s) to the victim and her/his family and answer their questions.

After hearing these choices outlined and processing the ramifications of each, the victim chooses which route to go. In the process of choosing, the victim may develop new questions she/he wants the offender to answer and may experience new feelings and emo-tions to be worked through with the victim's therapist. Among the options the victim has is changing her/his mind about closure choices at any time, including at the face-to-face meeting. Victims are invited to contact the V-SOT therapist-even years after the event- anytime they have questions or want to talk about the abuse experience.

The victim's therapist prepares the victim (and parents/guardian) for the meeting by reviewing questions and clarifying the family's expectations for the closure meeting. The therapist once again affirms for the victim that the offender is at fault and helps the victim choose how to make the meeting room feel as safe as possible, including favorite stuffed toys, seating arrangements, and so on.

The offender is prepared for the closure choice that the victim has made. The V-SOT therapist asks the offender the questions the victim has raised and relays answers if requested to by the victim. The "no-contact" contract is continued, the letters are sent, or the meeting is scheduled. The V-SOT therapist prepares the offender emotionally for the meeting if the victim has so chosen.

The goal of Stage 3 is to facilitate the most complete therapeutic closure possible around the abuse events, given the specific circumstances and personalities of all involved. A summary of the Victim-Sensitive Offender Therapy process appears in Table 1.

Case Study[6]

Michael is a 15-year-old boy who was living with his mother and 10-year-old brother in a college neighborhood. His parents had divorced eight years before, and his dad had moved to another state soon after. The children continued to see him for extended visits and on holidays. Michael's mother, Mindy, was an instructor in the college's English department and has been the custodial parent of Michael and his brother.

Michael had always been characterized as very family-centered, shy, and sensitive. He also was considered a good babysitter and regularly cared for the neighbors' 5-year-old girl, Tammy.

Suspicions were aroused when Tammy told her mother that her "gina" hurt, and her mother observed some irritation around Tammy's vaginal area. In answering questions, Tammy made it clear that Michael had been sexually abusing her under the rules of a "special and secret game."

---

6. This case history is a simplified composite. Babysitter-offenders may molest children in several of their client families, but in order to focus on the process, this history concentrates on just one victim family.

Shocked, Tammy's mother called Child Protection Services for advice. A social worker interviewed Tammy and there was a follow-up medical exam. The police interviewed Michael who, after considerable questioning, admitted a few instances of fondling. The police told Michael not to contact Tammy. The two families stopped communicating as well.

After Michael's limited offense disclosure, the courts sent Michael and his family to the PHASE Program for assessment. He and his family were accepted for the initial PHASE Assessment/Education Program. In Stage 1, during the first month of treatment, the therapist explained that releases of certain information were needed in order to do a complete assessment

---

Table 1
Overview of the Victim-Sensitive Offender Therapy Process

STAGE 1: "Switchboard" (Intake to 2 months)
A. Process for Offender:
  1. Offender (or guardian) signs releases of information for:
    a. Victim & offender's police/Child Protection statements.
    b. Permission to contact victim(s) (or parents/guardian).
B. Process for Victim:
  1. Initiate contact with victim (or parents/guardian). Answer questions, provide support for reporting, let them know disposition of case and offender's current status (i.e., on probation and in treatment).
  2. Discuss victim's need for treatment of abuse effects and provide current information and therapy referral.
  3. Solicit reports of offender's ongoing intrusive behavior and respond with appropriate measures to curb them.
  4. Explain purpose of release of information, request cooperation, and send release form to be signed by victim (or parents/guardian).
C. Goals:
  1. To complete a contextually sensitive offender assessment.
  2. To ensure a complete and therapeutic exchange of all abuse-relevant information among involved systems and persons.
  3. To establish the identity of the V-SOT therapist as the victim's advocate within the offender's milieu.
  4. To enlist victim's (et al.) involvement in the victim-sensitive offender therapy process.

STAGE 2: Confront Misattributions & Check Progress (3-5 months)
A. Process for offender:
  1. Check offender's misattributions toward victim(s) or system:
    a. Offender fully accepts blame/responsibility for acting on his decision to abuse.
    b. Offender clearly knows effects of abuse on victim.
    c. Offender owns full responsibility for abuse consequences to himself.
  2. Offender completes a "sexual abuse biography" and writes a clear "letter of apology" to the victim(s) (and victim's parents) for his abuse behavior.
B. Process for Victim:
  1. Check progress of victim therapy.
  2. Provide needed information and a progress report of offender to victim and/or guardians.
C. Goals:
  1. To confront any continued sexual abuse misattributions.
  2. To complete a progress assessment of the offender and victim.
  3. To revise the treatment plan and closure expectations in preparation for Stage 3.

Table 1 (continued)
Overview of the Victim-Sensitive Offender Therapy Process

STAGE 3: Closure Choices (6-12+ months)
A. Process for victim(s) (or parents):
  1. Choose closure option:
    a. The offender continues a "no contact" contract with the victim (and family).
    b. The offender mails a "letter of apology" to the victim.
    c. The offender attends a face-to-face closure meeting with the victim (and family), reads apology letter, answers questions.
  2. Prepare for closure:
    a. Process new questions and feelings.
    b. Clarify expectations.
    c. Choose ways to make the meeting room (if closure meeting is chosen)/home/neighborhood/school feel safe.
B. Process for offender (and family):
  1. Understand and comply with the expressed choices of the victim(s) (or parents).
C. Goals:
  1. Offender face the personal effects of his abusive behavior and make apology.
  2. Victim develop a sense of personal closure and control.

---

and to inform Tammy's parents that Michael and his family were involved in therapy. Michael and his mother signed releases of information for the therapist to receive copies of Michael's statements to the police. They also gave permission for the therapist to contact Tammy's parents in order to find out how Tammy and her parents were doing and to begin a potential process of healing.

After receiving the signed releases, the V-SOT therapist called Tammy's parents, Tom and Theresa, the next day. Theresa answered, and the V-SOT therapist explained who he was and let her know that Michael was currently in the assessment/ education phase of an adolescent sex-offender treatment program. He also explained that Michael and his mother had signed releases of information so the therapist could talk to Theresa and Tom about Michael's case.

Theresa said she was thankful the therapist had called because there had been no communication between the two families since the investigation three months before. The family had been concerned about how Michael was doing, whether Mindy was mad at them for reporting the abuse, and if there was any new information on what Michael had done to Tammy.

The therapist told Theresa that Michael was slowly opening up and that Mindy was not angry at them, but there was little new information on the abuse itself since Michael was just beginning the program. The therapist assured Theresa that she and Tom would receive new information as it came out in Michael's therapy.

Tom and Theresa shared information about Tammy's reactions to the abuse that had manifested since the initial investigation. Tammy had remembered more abuse incidents involving Michael. She had nightmares, enuresis, and phobias that appeared to be abuse-related. Tammy's parents asked for a therapy referral, saying that they were beginning to realize that the abuse had more of an effect on her-and on them-than they first thought. Theresa disclosed that she had been a victim of sexual abuse herself as a child; she worried about whether that had "contributed" to her not seeing or realizing that Tammy was being sexually abused. Torn wanted to know whether the *Playboy* magazines he had in the bedroom might have been used in Michael's abuse of Tammy.

The V-SOT therapist promised Torn and Theresa that this new information would be used in Michael's assessment and that their specific questions would be followed up in the course of Michael's therapy. They were referred to a victim-oriented therapist who was comfortable working with an "offender" therapist. The V-SOT therapist asked the family to sign release forms allowing him to get copies of Tammy's statements to the Child Protection Services worker. The victim therapist asked the family to sign releases of information so she could consult with the V-SOT therapist; after hearing why it was necessary, Torn and Theresa agreed to sign.

During Stage 2-Michael had been in treatment just over three months- Tammy disclosed more specific details of the abuse to her parents and therapist, who relayed the information to the V-SOT therapist. The V-SOT therapist confronted Michael with the new information, and he finally admitted a two-year history of regular sexual contact with Tammy, including fondling, oral sex, and "humping" Tammy until he ejaculated. Michael wrote an "abuse biography" detailing his new information on how he abused Tammy. He had, for example, abused Tammy in the bathroom, and this information helped explain Tammy's fear of the bathroom and her enuresis. After the V-SOT therapist shared this information with her therapist and parents, who talked about it with Tammy, her bathroom phobia and enuresis stopped.

Michael expressed increased remorse as he realized that his abusive actions were having long-term effects on Tammy and her family, as well as on him and his family. In addition, he clarified that while he did use one of Tom's *Playboy* magazines in the course of abusing Tammy, he had discovered them after he had already started his abuse behavior.

Michael was now able to write sincere letters of apology to Tammy and to Tom and Theresa (see Table 2). In family therapy, Michael made a heartfelt apology to his mother for all he had put her

---

Table 2
Michael's Letters of Apology

Dear Tammy,
I don't know what words to use. I'm sorry for sexually abusing you. It wasn't your fault in any way, it was all mine. It will never ever happen again to you or anyone else. I hope this letter will help in overcoming the bad experiences I put you through.

> Sincerely,
> *Michael*

Dear Mr. and Mrs. Smith,
I'm very sorry for sexually abusing your daughter. You don't have to believe me, and I will not go on and on and try to say I'm sorry the amount of times it would take to heal your wounds. I don't think there are any words that can describe the deep feeling of hate in my heart for the things I did. I really am very sorry, and I hope that in time you won't hate me. But if you do, I can't blame you. I did such a bad thing, I just can't express my feelings of how very sorry I really am.

> Sincerely,
> *Michael*

through. Mindy said she forgave him and told him she was satisfied with his progress so far. She also said she was glad to know that Tammy, Torn, and Theresa's needs were taken into consideration in the therapy process.

The V-SOT therapist contacted Tammy, Torn, and Theresa's therapist to give a progress report on Michael and to let the family know that they could receive his letters of apology at the end of Michael's therapy; if they wished. The victim's therapist reported that Theresa was dealing with her own childhood sexual abuse in the course of Tammy's victim therapy, but that Theresa's childhood sexual abuse trauma did not add an emotional burden to Tammy's experience. In fact, processing Tammy's experience of abuse was helping Theresa work through something she had buried for years.

The V-SOT therapist contacted Tom and Theresa, along with Tammy's therapist, to outline their closure options: continuing a no-contact contract, receiving Michael's letters of apology through the mail, or having a face-to-face process session with Michael. The V-SOT therapist offered to answer any detailed questions Tammy's therapist and her parents might have about their closure options. Tom and Theresa, after talking with Tammy's therapist and Tammy, decided they wanted a face-to-face meeting in their therapist's office.

The goals of Stage 2 were completed with the progress assessment of the offender and victim. The treatment plan and expectations were revised accordingly.

Michael was assessed as ready to prepare for closure. He was demonstrating remorse for his actions in the content of his abuse biography and letters, by complying with treatment plan and program contracts, and by expressing worry about Tammy's welfare. His language in therapy had shifted from blaming Tammy and Child Protection Services for his current problems to accepting responsibility for both his abusive actions and their consequences to himself. In fact, Michael went a little overboard, turning "accepting responsibility" into self-blame and self-hate. He became very de- pressed for a short time until he was reminded that while he had done something very wrong, he was now in the process of making amends. At this time, he rewrote and read his abuse biography and letters for the third time and they were accepted by his therapist, his mother, and his offender-treatment group. Michael's treatment plan was revised to focus on encouraging Michael to provide honest, open answers to the questions Tammy and her parents had asked and on preparing for the in-person closure meeting.

Tammy's therapist worked with her using play therapy, among other techniques, to create an environment safe enough for Tammy to talk more freely about Michael's abuse. Including Tammy's mother in some sessions was an important step in showing Tammy that despite what Michael had told her, she had not been "bad" and would not be punished or abandoned for breaking the secret-keeping rules of Michael's abuse "game." It was explained to Tammy that *Michael* broke the rules in making her play such a mean game with him and making her keep a secret that hurt her. Tammy expressed appropriate anger at Michael (represented by a male doll) for tricking her and making her keep "bad" secrets. The therapist prepared Tammy for not ever being alone with Michael because he had done a hurtful thing. When she expressed sadness that she wouldn't get to play the "good" games with Michael any more, the therapist explained that her friends and family couldn't be positive that he would never hurt her again, and they wanted to keep her safe. The therapist asked Tammy if she would like Michael to say he was sorry for tricking her and hurting her, and Tammy said yes. The therapist, Tammy, and her parents worked on some questions they wanted Michael to answer. The therapist relayed their questions to Michael's V-SOT therapist.

In Stage 3, after Michael had been in therapy for eight months, a meeting was arranged at Tammy's therapist's office. The meeting format was agreed on in consultation between her therapist and the V-SOT therapist. Michael would take the initiative in reviewing his abuse biography and answering any questions asked by Tom, Theresa, or Tammy. Michael was prepared for the meeting with role plays in his offender-treatment group. Tammy's therapist prepared her clients at the same time, working on their questions and what they could reasonably expect from the closure session.

Tammy and her parents arrived at their therapist's office half an hour before the scheduled meeting time so they could feel settled, comfortable, and in control before Michael, Mindy, and the V-SOT therapist arrived. Michael and his support people arrived and were seated facing Tammy's family and therapist. After the V-SOT therapist reviewed the structure of the meeting, Michael began. With the help of his therapist, Michael summarized his abuse biography. Michael and his therapist answered Tammy's, Tom's, and Theresa's questions as they arose. As Michael read his letter of apology to Tammy, he started to cry, saying he felt really bad because he sincerely liked Tammy and realized how he had used her affection for him to hurt her, as well as abusing Tom and Theresa's trust. Tammy appeared unmoved- she couldn't seem to believe that Michael, who had been in such a position of power over her, was reduced to tears and guilt. The V-SOT therapist offered Michael's letter of apology to her, and she accepted it. After she looked at the letter, Tammy asked her mother to hold it for safe keeping.

Michael read his other letter of apology to Tom and Theresa, who graciously accepted it. Tammy said that the abuse was not her fault, but Michael's, and her statement was confirmed, first by Michael and then by all the participants. She said she was glad he had gotten the help that he needed, especially because she had been worried he might do it to other little girls. Tom and Theresa were satisfied with the process and relieved to get information they needed. They also said that they forgave Michael. Mindy observed that she and Michael had grown as a result of facing Michael's abusive behavior.

The families discussed what level of contact between them would be appropriate in the future. They clarified that it will take some time to fully trust Michael but that they wished to continue to communicate as neighbors, with the parents freely exchanging phone calls. Both families agreed that Michael could never again be placed in a position of trust with Tammy. This session ended with handshakes, and a few weeks later Michael graduated from the PHASE Program.

Summary and Treatment Results

The present offender program was designed to be victim-sensitive throughout the treatment process. At the time of the initial assessment, the safety of the victim is put foremost during offender placement recommendations. Throughout the program language is encouraged which benefits the victim by confronting all offender misattributions and by teaching offenders to use self-responsible language. During the final closure choices, sensitivity to the victim involves restoring power and control through having the victim decide what type of closure will occur, and where and with whom it will take place.

The following is a retrospective summary of closure choices made in this treatment program over a three-year period, categorized by offense type. The closure method chosen can usually be predicted by the frequency of contact and degree of intimacy between the offender/ family and the victim/family.

Sexual Abuse within the Nuclear Family (Incest)

The vast majority of incest cases are resolved with a face-to-face closure meeting between the offender and his younger siblings. This is, of course, typical of the practice now used with family-based incest treatment programs. A handful end with the letter of apology (see Table 3), when the family has other abusive or very disorganized features, or the offender has been rejected by the family and is in an out-of-home placement.

Sexual Abuse by an Extended Family Member (Incest)

This type of sexual abuse typically occurs in a babysitting situation or family gathering, where an uncle or grandparent takes advantage of his niece/nephew or grand- child. The majority of these cases end with a face-to-face reconciliation meeting. The remain- der end with letters of apology (see Table 3), usually because the victim's family lives some distance from the offender's family and they have only occasional contact.

Sexual Abuse by a Neighbor

A minority of cases in this category resolve in face-to-face meetings. Those that do commonly involve the next-door neighbor, a close family friend, or others who live very near to the family and where there are firm social ties with regular contact. Less intimate relation- ships typically end with a letter of apology (see Table 3) because the victim's family wishes for a "less formal" resolution.

In addition, few cases involving babysitting by a neighborhood acquaintance (i.e., where the offender was a babysitter known to the community or the son of a daycare provider) end in face-to-face meetings. Since the relationship was simply functional, the victim's family usually severs all ties. Most choose to learn the details of the abuse through the V-SOT therapist and elect to receive a letter of apology through the mail. A significant minority of the families opt for a continued "no-contact" contract monitored by the V-SOT therapist and probation officer.

In a park or playground child molestation because there was no prior relationship with the offender, most victims choose to receive the letter of apology in the mail. When they are first contacted by the V-SOT therapist, most express thanks for being able to learn the results of their reporting the abuse. Again, a significant number of these families choose a continued "no-contact" contract and say they will keep the therapist's telephone number should any problems arise in the future.

The Non-touch Sex Offender

The category of "non-touch offender" includes those who steal underwear, expose their genitals, window-peep, or make obscene phone calls. If the underwear-stealing or exposing is against close family members, the cases necessarily resolve with face-to-face closure meetings. The meeting helps the victim to understand a behavior that seems bizarre and inexplicable.

Non-touch cases involving neighbors and strangers to the offender usually end with letters of apology (see Table 3) received through the mail. The V-SOT therapist answers the victim's questions and offers explanations of the offender's behavior to help put some of the victim's concerns to rest. The following letters were written by adolescent sex offenders who participated in the PHASE Program. They are illustrative letters with some names and details changed in order to protect the privacy of the clients.

Table 3
Apology Letter Examples

Brother-Sister Incest: These letters were written by a 15-year-old boy to his 5-year-old sister and his parents.

Dear Nancy,
I am very sorry for sexually abusing you. I took advantage of a trust that should not have been broken. This isn't at all your fault; it's mine. It will never happen again, because I love you and am getting help from Walter and the guys in the group.
  Love,
  Your Brother,
  David

Dear Mom and Dad,
I'm very sorry for sexually abusing Nancy. I know it was hard on you both and still is. It will never happen again because of the help I am receiving from Walter and the group; but the main reason is because I love you both and I don't want to hurt you or Nancy again.
  Love,
  Your Son,
  David

Extended Family Sexual Abuse: The apology letter below was written by a 16-year-old uncle to his 6-year-old niece who had trusted and loved him and feared he was angry at her for breaking the abuse secret.

Dear Becky,
I'm sorry. I'm sorry that I sexually abused you. There are a few things I want you to know. First of all, I'm not mad at you for telling others about what I did to you. What happened was not your fault, and in this way, I will be able to get some help straightening myself out. What I did to you was very wrong, and the counseling I'm receiving now is helping me to realize that.
  Sincerely,
  Matt

Table 3 (continued)
Apology Letter Examples

Exposer: The letter below was written by a 17-year-old male to a 34- year-old woman to whom he had exposed himself from his car in a parking lot.

Dear Janet,
I feel that you have the right to an apology from me. I honestly don't know exactly how to begin apologizing for the terrible episode I caused you. I have no explanation to offer you for what I did. You mustn't take it personally, because you did nothing to cause my actions. You were only an innocent victim. I know I've caused you a great deal of pain. It must have been very shocking to you. I feel that I have directly insulted you, and I know you were very offended. I hope you can accept my apology, and even if you don't, I can understand that. [...][7] It was my personal problem only. The legal system has helped me very much. I have learned many things through being given information and getting counseling. I've learned better morals and respect. Right now, I have a better under- standing of myself and other things that can help me control or even completely diminish my problem. I'm going to try very hard to put this all behind me and get started on the right track toward a better life.
   I'm very, very sorry.
   Brian

Fetish Burglar: The apology letter below is from a 16-year-old fetish burglar who stole underwear from his mother. She had been quite frightened by her son's behavior because she discovered her cut-up underwear under her son's bed. In time he was able to explain that he cut the underwear's leg holes so that he could get them over his large thighs in order to cross-dress, not as an angry act against his mom.

Dear Mom,
I am sorry for what I did, and I am sorry for all the pain and fear that I caused for you. As you know I am getting help for my problem of cross-dressing and stealing women's clothes. I feel I am making progress with this problem as well as with our relationship. I promise that it will never happen again but I also know that there is nothing I can say to get rid of the grief. I hope to prove that in time that you can again love and trust me.
   Love,
   Ned

Group-Influenced Offender[8]

The victims of this type of abuse are typically peers to the offenders. The abuse occurs in a group setting, such as a party, school bathroom, playground, or sporting event. Characteristically, the teenage offenders blame the victim through the attribution processes already referred to. The victim usually feels humiliated and confused. Peer gossip and rumor tend to isolate the victim further. As a result of the situational and attributional processes involved, all of these cases

---

7.   The brackets indicate removal of identifying information to protect the confidentiality of the client.
8.   In group assaults it is often difficult to get a specific offender prosecuted or convicted unless there were additional witnesses or one of the offenders agrees to testify against the rest.

end with an emotionally distant letter of apology, supplemented by a detailed explanation from the V-SOT therapist. Many victims in these situations move to new schools and neighborhoods in an attempt to sever all ties and escape the lingering social impact of the abuse.[9]

The Acquaintance Rapist

The victims of "date-rape" are generally very angry and traumatized by the forced sexual abuse event. They usually express relief that the offender is in treatment and anger about the assault, the legal process, and the emotional aftermath. Since the victim's experience is typically very different from the story the offender tells, the therapist can then use that information to confront the offender. Some victims accept a letter of apology from the offender on the condition it is sincere, and *all* request an assured "no-contact" contract.

---

9. While it hardly seems like justice that the therapist must take up the slack in accepting responsibility on the offenders' behalf, the process does maintain sensitivity to the victim's need for information, safety, and, when appropriate, resolution.

References

Bateson, G. (1972). *Steps to an ecology of mind.* New York: Ballantine Books.

Bera, W. (1985). *A preliminary investigation of a typology of adolescent sex offenders and their family systems.* Unpublished master's thesis, University of Minnesota.

Bera, W. (1980). *Self-defense/ assertiveness training in the treatment of sexual assault trauma.* Monograph available from the author.

Briere, J. (1984, April). *The effects of childhood sexual abuse on later psychological functioning: De- fining a post-sexual abuse syndrome.* Paper presented at the Third National Conference on Sexual Victimization of Children. Children's Hospital National Medical Center, Washington, D.C.

Burgess, A.W., & Holmstrom, L.L. (1975). Sexual trauma of children and adolescents: Sex, pressure, and secrecy. *Nursing Clinics of North America, IO,* 551-563.

Finkelhor, D. (1984). *Child sexual abuse: New theory and research.* New York: The Free Press.

Gelinas, D.J. (1988). Family therapy: Characteristic family constellations and basic therapeutic stance. In S. M. Sgroi, *Vulnerable populations: Evaluation and treatment of sexually abused children and adult survivors* (Vol. 1). Lexington, MA: Lexington Books.

Gilmartin, Z.P. (1983). Attribution theory and rape victim responsibility. *Deviant Behaviour, 4*(3- 4), 357-374.

Goodwin, J. (1982). *Sexual abuse: Incest victims and their families.* Boston, MA: John Wright.

Green, S. (1984). Survivor-offender reconciliation pro- gram: A review of the concept. *Social Action and the Law, 10*(2), 43-52.

Gulotta, G., & deCataldo-Neuberger, L. (1983). A systematic and attributional approach to victimology. *Victimology: An International Journal, 8,* 5-16.

Heider, F. (1958). *The psychology of interpersonal relations.* New York: Wiley.

Keller, E. (1980). *Sexual assault: A statewide problem.* Minnesota Program for Victims of Sexual Assault (LEAA Grant #4317013675). St. Paul, MN: Minnesota Department of Corrections.

Kelley, H., & Thibaut, J. (1969). Group problem solving. In G. Lindzey & E. Aronson (Eds.), *Handbook of social psychology* (Vol. 4, 2nd ed., pp. 1-101). Reading, MA: Addison- Wesley.

Knopp, F.H., Boward, B., Brach, M.J., Christianson, S., Largen, M.A., Lewin, J., Lugo, J., Morris, M., & Newton, W. (1976). *Instead of prisons.* Orwell, VT: The Safer Society Press.

Landis, J.T. (1956). Experiences of 500 children with adult sexual deviation. *Psychiatric Quarterly Supplement, 30,* 91-109.

Lerner, M. (1980). *The belief in a just world: A fundamental delusion.* New York: Plenum Press.

Mathews, R., Matthews, J., & Speltz, K. (1989). *Fe- male sex offenders: An exploratory study.* Orwell, VT: The Safer Society Press.

Monahan, J. (Ed.). (1980). *Who is the client? The ethics of psychological intervention in the criminal justice system.* Washington, DC: Ameri- can Psychological Association.

O'Brien, M. (1989). *Characteristics of adolescent male sibling incest offenders: Preliminary findings.* Orwell, VT: The Safer Society Press.

O'Brien, M., & Bera, W. (1986, Fall). Adolescent sex offenders: A descriptive typology. *Preventing Sexual Abuse, 1*(3), pp. 1-4.

Peters, J.J., Meyer, L.C., & Carroll, N.E. (1976). *The Philadelphia assault victim study.* (Final Re- port: National Institute of Mental Health, Center for Studies in Crime and Delinquency, Grant #R0IMH21304.) Philadelphia, PA: Philadelphia General Hospital Center for Rape Concern.

Peterson, J.J. (1976). Children who are victims of sexual assault and the psychology of offenders. *American Journal of Psychotherapy, 30,* 398-421.

Schoener,G., Milgrom, J., Gonsiorek, J., Luepker, E., & Conroe, R. (1989). *Psychotherapists' sexual involvement with clients: Intervention and prevention.* Minneapolis, MN: Walk-In Counseling Center.

Scully, D., & Marolla, J. (1984). Convicted rapists' vocabulary of motive: Excuses and justifications. *Social Problems, 31*(5), 530-544.

Sgroi, S.M. (1975, May-June). Sexual molestation of children: The last frontier in child abuse. *Children Today, 4*(3), 19-44.

Shotland, R.L., & Goodstein, L. (1983). Just because she doesn't want to doesn't mean it's rape: An experimentally based causal model of the perception of rape in a dating situation. *Social Psychology Quarterly, 45(3)*, 220-232.

Sutherland, E.H., & Cressey, D.R. (1978). *Criminology.* New York: J.B. Lippincott.

Umbreit, M. (1985). *Crime and reconciliation: Creative options for victims and offenders.* Nashville, TN: Abington Press.

Waterman, C.K., & Foss-Goodman, D. (1984). Child- molesting: Variables relating to attribution of fault to victims, offenders, and non-participating parents. *Journal of Sex Research, 20(4),* 329-349.

Wright, M., & Galaway, B. (Eds.). (1989). *Mediation and criminal justice: Victims, offenders and community.* Newbury Park, CA: Sage Publications.

Zehr, H. (1990). *Changing lenses: A new focus for crime and justice.* Scottsdale, AZ: Herald Press.

Umbreit, M. (1985). *Crime and reconciliation: Cre-ative options for victims and offenders.* Nashville, TN: Abington Press.

Waterman, C.K., & Foss-Goodman, D. (1984). Child- molesting: Variables relating to attribution of fault to victims, offenders, and non-participating parents. *Journal of Sex Research, 20(4),* 329-349.

Wright, M., & Galaway, B. (Eds.). (1989). *Mediation and criminal justice: Victims, offenders and community.* Newbury Park, CA: Sage Publi-cations.

Zehr, H. (1990). *Changing lenses: A new focus for crime and justice.* Scottsdale, AZ: Herald Press.

Chapter 4
THE CLINICAL EVALUATION MODEL: EMOTIONAL RESTITUTION TRAINING

James M. Yokley[1]

Abstract

This social responsibility treatment component emphasizes the need for careful evaluation of survivor-offender communication interventions and integrates survivor protection measures into a framework that can be used to evaluate which types of survivor-offender communications are safe and/or beneficial to the participants. This treatment develops offender responsibility towards survivors by exposing offenders to a series of survivor-trauma understanding interventions arranged in a hierarchy of increasing cognitive/affective impact on the offender. Offenders who demonstrate appropriate behavior during this graduated exposure receive permission to begin a series of gradually more direct survivor-offender communication interventions where the goal is to demonstrate responsible and prosocial behavior towards survivors. In the final intervention, offenders make emotional restitution, apologize, take full responsibility and explain their behavior to their specific survivors. This treatment incorporates psychological testing to monitor survivors who participate in direct interactions with offenders. The test results have thus far revealed no adverse impact on survivors involved in several types of survivor-offender communication interventions. This treatment component can be integrated into existing offender treatment programs.

Introduction and Treatment Philosophy

Emotional Restitution Training (ERT) is one of six social responsibility components in the Treatment for Appropriate Social Control (TASC) program. The TASC program was originally developed for outpatient treatment of youth offenders with sexually abusive behavior under age 21 considered to be a low to moderate risk for re-offense.

The primary goal of the overall TASC program is to decrease the offender's potential to reoffend by helping them: (1) increase their understanding of the cognitive/behavioral/ social process which led to and maintained the offense behavior pattern; (2) learn to understand the full impact of their behavior on others as well as the consequences of re-offense behavior; and (3) develop the skills necessary to control their own behavior and engage in appropriate relationships. TASC treatment components include: developing the offender's honesty and acceptance of responsibility for the offense (accurate self-monitoring and reporting of past and present behaviors); developing an understanding of the chain of events and decisions involved in the offense etiology; Emotional Restitution Training; prosocial decision making (moral development); arousal management training; and prosocial skills training. Offenders have the social responsibility to disclose everyone that they have victimized so that an effort to get them treatment can be made. When referring to their victim list, offenders the personal responsibility to respect those they have victimized as "survivors" of their sexual abuse.

---

1. Special thanks go to Denise McGuire for her work with many of the offenders who received this treatment which in the past has also been referred to as "Victim Responsibility Training"

Offenders participate in the TASC program for a period ranging from 18-to-30 months, depending on individual progress. The program involves two hours per week of group therapy and at least one hour of individual/family treatment every other week. Parents of offenders sign a form that indicates their consent to treatment and explains the limits of confidentiality on behalf of the offender (including consent to audio/video taping of sessions). Offenders sign a contract specifying that they will comply with group rules. Group treatment sessions are videotaped and offenders are informed that the tapes may be used in individual/ family sessions (to help deal with denial, responsibility, and supervision issues) and to train therapists. To decrease the probability of physical aggression during emotionally charged sessions, offenders are reminded that their behavior is being videotaped and informed that tapes of their group rule violations will be shown to their guardians/parents, probation officers, or human services case workers.

The TASC program philosophy is based on a "clinical evaluation" model, which recognizes that since the field of sex-offender evaluation and intervention is currently in the development stages, the procedures employed should be evaluated and documented objectively. Such documentation can provide results that are useful in formulating sex-offender research projects to evaluate the procedures employed and improve the next intervention trial.

Given this philosophy, the goals of the clinical evaluation model are to develop theory-based interventions with operationally defined concepts and to document their course using the most rigorous evaluation methods possible. The clinical evaluation model advocates the use of quasi-experimental clinical evaluation trials, single-case designs, and the "events paradigm." [2]

The first two TASC treatment components train the offender to develop honesty about offenses, understand their offense behavior, cope with deviant thoughts appropriately, and accept their survivor safety standards. Emotional Restitution Training (ERT) begins when offenders have been in treatment for 8 to 12 months and teaches the offender to understand their survivor's thoughts and feelings in order to act responsibly toward the survivor of their sexually abusive behavior. Only offenders who successfully complete the first two TASC treatment components are allowed to begin this phase of treatment. All case studies and clinical evaluation data reported are based on clients who were in treatment over the past two calendar years.

A primary objective of ERT is to protect survivors who participate in the process from further emotional trauma. Offenders have to earn permission to communicate responsibly with survivors by going through graduated levels of responsibility training. Each step of their progress in demonstrating their survivor understanding and ability to behave responsibly is evaluated before they are allowed to go on to the next step.

---

2. Sex-offender interventions are primarily conducted in applied settings that, by their nature, prevent the controlled, comparative clinical trials needed for traditional research studies. Examples of quasi-experimental methods of documenting treatment change are explained by Riecken and Boruch (1974). Kazdin (1975) provides examples of the various single-case methods of documenting treatment change and the events paradigm" which examines the psychological changes produced by brief treatment segments, is described in Elliot, Reimschuessel, Cislo, & Sack (1985).

Treatment Description

ERT consists of eight consecutive cognitive-behavioral interventions on two separate social responsibility levels. The first level develops the offenders' understanding of the impact of their behavior on the survivor. Level 1 of ERT addresses the offender's cognitive/affective problem areas and was designed to help the offender understand the survivor's thoughts and feelings. Some of the procedures used in Level 1 of this process are referred to as "victim empathy" training in other sex-offender programs (Knopp, 1982). Having problems with empathy for others "is the hallmark of the perpetrator of child sexual abuse" and "simplifies abuse of power because failure to perceive the negative consequences of exploitation of the victim diminishes or even eliminates guilt for the perpetrator" (Sgroi, 1982, p. 253). Level 2 teaches the offender to develop socially responsible interpersonal skills and to demonstrate prosocial behaviors towards survivors.

One current treatment premise is that adolescent sex offenders who lack social responsibility and appropriate social behavior control also lack appropriate cognitions and affect regarding the problems their behaviors cause others. Their dysfunctional cognitions and maladaptive self-statements rationalizing, justifying, or minimizing the effects that offenders have on others are thought to contribute to this deficit (Knopp, 1982). The offender's inaccurate perceptions and faulty attributions (i.e., cognitive distortions) that blame the offender's behavior on others or attribute that behavior to external factors are also considered contributing factors. In order to modify offenders' maladaptive self-statements and cognitive distortions regarding survivor abuse, offender programs typically use interventions with bibliotherapy prompts (i.e., articles about or letters by survivors), live or videotaped psychoeducational presentations (i.e., where survivors or survivor therapists speak about the abuse), or various types of role playing (Knopp, 1984).

Level 1 of ERT is based on the theory that the offender's lack of appropriate cognitions towards their survivors represents an *affective avoidance response.* The Sex Of- fender Therapy Program at the Echo Glen Children's Center in Snoqualmie, Washington, also held the belief that many offenders have the *capacity* for thought and concern about the problems their behaviors cause others but *avoid* it because of the considerable anxiety and guilt it elicits (Knopp, 1982). Distress caused by empathic over-arousal may create an aversive state that overwhelms an individual's distress tolerance. Cognitive functions *impeding* empathy and *decreasing* the offender's probability of taking prosocial action may then occur. For example, the distressed person may become self-focused and preoccupied with the aversive state or make a causal attribution (e.g., blaming the survivor) to reduce their level of discomfort (Palmer, 1989).

The four interventions in Level 1 of Emotional Restitution Training are presented in a hierarchy of increasing cognitive/affective impact on the offender in an attempt to prevent affective avoidance responses. In group therapy sessions, offenders are gradually introduced to more emotionally charged presentations of the impact of their behavior on their survivors. This form of graduated exposure is referred to as *"in vivo* group flooding," the gradual in- crease in group exposure to an aversive stimulus without permitting escape. Both exposure and flooding techniques are considered readily adaptable for use with groups of clients facing similar fears (Emmelkamp, 1982; Michelson, 1985). To develop offender understanding of the survivor, Ross and Loss

(1988) have recommended different forms of the first three types of Level 1 interventions.

Group discussions of offender reactions follow each of the four Level 1 cognitive- behavioral interventions. During these discussions, response modeling, feedback, and verbal reinforcement techniques are employed. In addition, positive peer models are verbally praised, while offenders expressing maladaptive cognitions and inappropriate affective responses are confronted by both therapists and positive peer models.

After completing each of the four Level 1 interventions (described below), all offenders rate the effects of that intervention on a 22-question offender-impact questionnaire (see Appendix B-1).

Emotional Restitution Training Level 1
Intervention 1
The first ERT intervention uses a bibliotherapy assignment in which offenders read two newspaper articles about the impact of sexual abuse on survivors. The first news article describes the types of thoughts and feelings that survivors experience and how their trauma is often revived by news of sexual assaults. The second news article describes the trauma suffered by a specific survivor of a serial rapist who was not charged because he was caught after the statute of limitations on his crime expired.[3] After the group discusses these articles, all offenders complete an offender-impact questionnaire and work on a graded homework assignment where they answer six questions on the articles.

Intervention 2
The second intervention involves a bibliotherapy prompt procedure where the offenders hear actual letters written by unrelated survivors about their abuse. Three letters written by survivors are read to the offender groups by their therapists. The first letter was written by a teenage female incest survivor (in treatment at a local agency program for survivors) to the offender (her stepfather). In it, she expresses her specific feelings directly towards her offender: "Dear Rick, I hate your guts. You're a fat ugly toad. I don't know where you get off thinking you could get away with..." The second letter (written by the same incest survivor to her unassertive, enabling mother) again expresses specific feelings directly toward the target person: "Dear Terri, You always asked me what it was you were doing wrong in raising your children, well now I'm going to tell you..."[4] The third letter was written by a "Hilcrest student" (reprinted from Ross & Loss, 1988, Appendix VI), and describes how sexually abused survivors feel, targeting all offenders collectively. After the group discusses these articles, all offenders again fill out the offender-impact questionnaire and complete another six-question homework assignment.

Intervention 3
In the third intervention, offenders observe an emotionally charged videotape of the impact of sexual abuse on survivors. Although high-quality dramatic television programs on the impact of sexual abuse have been produced, in order to avoid triggering maladaptive self-statements which

---

3. The news articles-discussed were from the *Akron Beacon Journal* (9/4/88) entitled "News of rape often revives victim's terror, guilt feelings" and "Stark rape victim anguishes over prosecution loophole."
4. Letters are used in the offender treatment group by permission of the victim who wrote them.

discount the information being given, ERT uses a videotape depicting real survivors of sexual abuse who discuss the actual abuse events that occurred as well as their real thoughts and feelings about being abused.[5] This videotape describes the trauma of four sexual abuse survivors, two females and two males. The first survivor, who was molested by both her father and grandfather, makes a statement particularly important to the preparation of offenders for responsible behavior towards their survivors:

My grandfather died before I had the chance to go back and confront him about what he did to me. I determined that I wasn't going to let that happen with my father...It was real important to give him back his burden. I needed something from him. I needed him to say "I did it and I'm sorry" and to really recognize what he had done to me.

After group discussion of the survivor videotape, all offenders again complete offender-impact questionnaires.

Intervention 4
In the fourth intervention, offenders attend a Survivor Impact session somewhat similar to the survivor-impact panels used by Mothers Against Drunk Drivers to confront drunk driving offenders.[6]

A Survivor-offender Reconciliation Group was established recently in the largest prison in the free world at Vacaville, California. This group brings offenders "face to face with survivors so that they can face and free themselves" (Pollak, 1990). The Vacaville group uses the survivor impact-panel approach where survivors come into the prison and speak directly to the offenders about their victimization and the impact of the crime on their lives. The group has met once a week for the past 18 months. Among the first to meet the offenders were three survivors of brutal rapes. One of the survivors said, "You have to put faces on the survivors and you have to put faces on the offenders before anything can change." One of the offenders concurred, saying, "When I started thinking about this person's parents, their mother and father and how I would feel if it would have been my dad or my sister or somebody close to me like that, it made me want to cry, it really hurt me deep inside and made me want to think of doing something to repay it."

In the Survivor Impact Session employed in ERT Intervention 4, adolescent survivors of sexual

---

5. "The videotape used was *Surviving Sexual Abuse,* University of California Extension Media Center, 2176 Shattuck Ave., Berkeley, CA 94704, (415) 642-0460. Pollak (1990) recently produced a brief television documentary of a Survivor-offender Reconciliation Group which also utilizes a videotape of five survivors of different crimes to help incarcerated criminals visualize what they have done to others.
6. "While no previous data are available on the benefits of impact sessions for sexual abuse survivors and their offenders, Lord (1989) reports that this intervention is valuable both tor victims of drunk driving and their offenders. Parents of those killed by drunk driving offenders are overcome by grief and suffer the helplessness and powerlessness that sex abuse survivors experience. According to Lord, drunk driving victims serving on an impact panel experienced a decrease in distressful feelings after telling their story, a positive feeling of increased personal strength after the emotionally draining panel, and a belief that they may be preventing the victimization of others. Impact panels are reported to help offenders move beyond focusing on their own consequences to considering the pain that their behavior has caused others, break down denial that they have a problem, imprint cognitive images of real people suffering to recall when reoffending is an option, and change their behavior.

abuse from a local agency's survivor treatment program volunteer to address the offender group. These survivors describe the sexual abuse committed against them and give direct feedback to the offenders on the specific impact that sexual abuse has had on their lives. The survivors may then ask the offenders to disclose their offenses, to explain why they offended, and to answer any other questions. This intervention's goals are to help survivors decrease their emotional distress by getting answers to their questions about offender thoughts and behaviors and to develop offenders' understanding of the impact of their abuse behavior.

The Survivor Impact Session is the first opportunity for offender-therapists to observe responsible offender behavior in the presence of a survivor. During the Survivor Impact Session, therapists sit on both sides of the survivors so that no survivor is sitting next to an offender in the group. Offenders are prepared for the meeting with discussions of responsible and appropriate behavior towards the survivors conducting the impact session. The desired offender behaviors towards the survivors before, during, and after the session are specified in a 10-item written behavior contract (see Appendix B-2). They go into the meeting with the understanding that they *owe* emotional restitution to survivors, and that they have a responsibility to make an honest attempt to answer whatever questions survivors ask them. During the impact session, which is held in the offenders' group meeting room, survivors are seated so the video camera films the offenders, not the survivors.

While the main focus of ERT interventions is on changing the offenders' thoughts, feelings, and behaviors, protecting survivors from being further traumatized receives equal attention and care. To monitor whether survivor volunteers experience any adverse impact from facing offenders, the program evaluates the effects of survivor participation on impact panels by administering psychological tests to survivor panelists before and after the panel presentation. Survivor volunteers are asked to complete the Beck Depression Inventory (Beck & Steer, 1987), the State-Trait Anxiety Inventory (Spielberger, 1983), and the Rotter Internal-External Locus of Control Scale (Rotter, 1966). In addition, all survivor volunteers are asked to complete a "Thoughts and Feelings Questionnaire" (see Appendix B-3) to evaluate the subjective impact of the session on the survivor volunteers in other areas. [7]

Offenders discuss the Survivor Impact Session and complete offender-impact questionnaires but are not monitored with psychological testing during this intervention.[8] An outline of Level 1 interventions appears in Table 1.

---

7. The purpose of the tests is explained verbally to the survivor panelists ("We need to find out whether this session is going to affect you in some way that's not obvious, so we can get you extra help if it does"), and they give verbal consent to the testing. The test results are given to their therapist and become part of their treatment charts. A panelist who declined to be tested would be recommended not to participate in the panel. While in theory a panelist could refuse to be tested after the Survivor Impact Session, that has not happened to date.

8. Offenders who serve as panelists before a group of survivors in treatment are monitored with psychological testing during that intervention (see Intervention 8, the Offender Information Group).

Table 1
Treatment Model for Emotional Restitution Training

Level 1: Developing Survivor Impact Understanding
(4 interventions used to prepare the offender to communicate responsibly with survivors)

Intervention 1	Intervention 2	Intervention 3	Intervention 4
Newspaper Articles on survivors	Letters by survivors	Survivor video tape	Survivor Impact (1) Session
questionnaire; group discussion; graded paper	questionnaire; group discussion; graded paper	questionnaire; group discussion	questionnaire; group discussion

◄──────── **COGNITIVE/AFFECTIVE IMPACT** ────────►

Level 2: Emotional Restitution
(4 prosocial behavior interventions involving therapeutic survivor-offender communication)

Intervention 5	Intervention 6	Intervention 7	Intervention 8
Letters to indirect victims (2)	Apology to indirect victims (3)	Letters to direct victims (4)	Apology to direct victims (1,4)
group grade	questionnaire	group grade	OR
			Offender Information Group (5)
			Questionnaire

◄──────── **INTERPERSONAL** ────────►

Note: Offender tasks are listed under each intervention

1. Survivor(s) emotional state (i.e., level of depression, anxiety, and external control) is evaluated before and after contact with offenders.
2. Telephone feedback on survivor impact is gathered after this intervention.
3. Impact questionnaire on the apology letter and session is given to indirect survivor.
4. Impact questionnaires are given to survivor and his/her therapist after this intervention.
5. Both survivor(s) and offenders' emotional state are evaluated before and after group contact with each other.

Emotional Restitution Training Level 2

Since sexual abuse often leaves survivors feeling guilty and culpable, the second level of ERT consists of four *prosocial behavior interventions* (interventions 5 through 8) requiring the offender to relieve the survivor of that burden by holding themselves responsible to the survivor for their offense. Level 2 of ERT gradually shapes offenders' acceptance of full responsibility for their crimes.

The format is based on the theory that the transfer of responses from a *training* situation to the *target* situation is improved when the training situation is similar to the target situation. Role playing, behavior rehearsal, performance feedback, and verbal praise move the offender along a graduated sequence of four prosocial behavior interventions culminating in the offender accepting full responsibility for the abuse in an apology session with their direct survivor. ERT Level 2 uses behavioral observation of what the offender has learned along with the psychological testing and self-reports of survivors to measure whether survivor-offender interactions have any adverse impact on survivors.

Intervention 5

In the fifth intervention, the offender writes an apology letter to individuals other than their survivor(s) who have also been affected by their crime. Since family members (especially parents) often experience feelings of anxiety, guilt, or shame over the victimization, in most cases at least one family member can be defined as an indirect survivor of the offender's crime. The designated indirect survivor is preferably a parent or adult who has not sexually offended or been sexually victimized.

The offender is required to write an apology letter to the indirect survivor(s) and read that letter to the group. The group discusses the letter, and offenders who model responsible written statements toward their indirect survivors are verbally praised, while offenders expressing maladaptive cognitions and inappropriate affective responses are confronted by both therapists and positive peer models. After this feedback session each member in the group gives the offender's letter a grade, the average is computed, and a group grade is assigned. If the grade is below a "B" or the therapists feel that important changes are needed, the offender is instructed to use the feedback to modify the letter and to present the letter to the group again. This feedback loop between the offender and the group continues until the offender's written expression has been appropriately shaped. This feedback loop is useful in remediating the offender's survivor-understanding deficits remaining after the completion of ERT Level 1.

After the offender completes their letter and receives a satisfactory grade from the offender group, the offender's therapist contacts the indirect survivor by telephone. The therapist explains the apology letter process and asks whether the indirect survivor would like to receive an apology in the mail. If the indirect survivor chooses to receive the apology letter, it is sent along with an explanation of the apology process (see Appendix A) and a two-page brief review of why adolescents molest. This information is provided to empower family members in their struggle to understand and cope with the behavior of the offender.

Several days after the apology letter is sent, the therapist again contacts the indirect survivor(s) by telephone and asks if they found the letter to be sincere and helpful. The therapist and the indirect survivor discuss the impact of the letter and decide whether to schedule an apology session with the offender. If the apology letter is judged sincere and helpful by both the indirect survivor and the offender's therapist, and if the indirect survivor chooses to meet with the offender, then the offender is allowed to apologize to the indirect survivor in person. The appropriateness of the offender's behavior during that session is evaluated (Intervention 6) to determine whether the offender will be allowed to write an apology letter to their direct survivor(s).

If the indirect survivor (or the direct survivor) chooses not to meet with the offender, the offender participates in an Offender Information Group for survivors.

Intervention 6
In the sixth intervention, the offender apologizes in person to their indirect survivor(s). This intervention acts as a "training" apology session where the therapist conducts a behavioral observation of how the offender handles an apology session, and the offender receives performance feedback along with verbal reinforcement. Appropriate behavior is required before the offender has any contact with their direct survivor. After the apology session with their indirect survivor(s), the offender completes an offender-impact questionnaire. During this time, the indirect survivor is asked to complete a follow-up questionnaire on the impact that the apology letter and the apology session had on him or her (see Appendix C-1). If the offender's apology session behavior with the indirect survivor is judged appropriate and helpful by both the indirect survivor and the offender's therapist, then the offender is allowed to write an apology letter to their direct survivor.

If the offender behaves inappropriately, he is not allowed to contact their direct survivor and undergoes additional therapy. If the indirect survivor and the therapist disagree on their evaluation of the offender's behavior, the indirect survivor's feedback is reviewed, and the offender is not allowed to proceed with writing their apology letter to the direct survivor until both the indirect survivor and the offender's therapist consider it appropriate. If warranted, the offender's therapist may recommend treatment to help the indirect survivor deal with unresolved issues.

Intervention 7
In the seventh intervention, offenders who handle their apology to the indirect survivor responsibly use the skills developed during the previous six interventions to write apology letters to their direct survivors. Apology letters to direct survivors are also utilized in the Twelve Step Guide for Healing from Compulsive Sexual Behavior *(Hope and Recovery,* 1987). Step nine of this guide requires offenders to make direct amends to their survivors wherever possible, except when to do so would injure them or others. [9]

9. The method of ascertaining whether direct amends would injure others outlined in *Hope and Recovery* has offenders write letters acknowledging previous harm they'd caused, then calling the recipient to ask for a reaction. The ERT method, while similar, protects the survivor from intrusive contact by the offender in having the offender's therapist make contact and having the offender go through six closely monitored responsibility training interventions before any direct survivor contact is allowed by letter or in person.

The apology letter is discussed and modified in a feedback loop with the offender group in the same manner as the letter to the indirect survivor in Intervention 5. Prosocial survivor behaviors are modeled by offenders whose letters fully accept responsibility for the crime, acknowledge that getting reported or arrested was needed and helpful, and convey their genuine sorrow for specific emotional/physical damage done to the survivor. These offenders receive verbal praise and high group grades. [10]

After the offender completes their direct-survivor apology letter and it receives a satisfactory grade from the offender group, the group therapist contacts the survivor's therapist by telephone to explain the apology letter process and alert the survivor's therapist that the apology letter is being mailed to him/her. The decision regarding whether to give the survivor the apology letter is left up to the survivor's therapist in consultation with the survivor. If the survivor's therapist and the survivor agree that the survivor can receive the letter without harm and/or that the letter will be therapeutic, the therapist presents and discusses the letter in therapy. The impact of the letter is evaluated using follow-up questionnaires enclosed with the apology letter. One is completed by the survivor and the other completed by the survivor's therapist (these are similar, but not identical to the questionnaire in Appendix C-2).

If the apology letter is judged sincere and helpful by the survivor, the survivor's therapist, and the offender's therapist, and if the survivor gives informed consent to a meeting with the offender, then the offender is allowed to apologize to the survivor in a therapy session. Every attempt is made to include both the offender and survivor therapists in the actual apology session (Intervention 8).[11]

Intervention 8

The eighth and last ERT intervention takes one of two courses. If the letter to the actual (direct) survivor was judged appropriate and helpful by both the survivor and the survivor's therapist, and if the survivor chooses to meet with the offender, then the offender is allowed to apologize in person to the survivor in a therapy session. Apology sessions to direct survivors are also utilized by the Twelve Step program for healing compulsive sexual behavior, which requires offenders to make direct amends to their survivors wherever it is possible, when it is not likely to injure others and where the survivor agrees to a meeting *(Hope and Recovery,* 1987). In ERT, the meeting is scheduled at the child mental health center, already a familiar place to both survivor and offender. If the survivor's caretaker, therapist, or advocate predicts that a direct apology session would traumatize the survivor or if the survivor declines the apology session, the offender must conduct an Offender Information Group for members of a survivor treatment group.

---

10. It is also expected that offenders will demonstrate feelings of shame and disgust over their abusive behavior, but such feelings are not necessarily included in direct survivor letters.

11. If the survivor has no therapist currently, the prospective session is carefully reviewed, and depending on the survivor's stability, is not held, postponed until the survivor is in therapy (or has the support of a suitable survivor advocate), or held with only the offender-therapist present. In the latter case, the offender-therapist assumes more explicitly the role of the survivor's advocate.

When an apology session is scheduled, the direct survivor is asked to complete a series of psychological tests one week before and after the apology session to monitor feelings of depression, anxiety, and feeling externally controlled, as in Intervention 4.[12]

Given that Intervention 8 involves an individual survivor facing her/his specific offender (as opposed to a group of survivors who support each other while facing a group of offenders who did not assault them), the level of survivor monitoring is increased by adding a measure of survivor anger, the State-Trait Anger Expression Inventory (Spielberger, 1988) to measures of depression, anxiety and external control.[13]

The impact of the offender's apology session with their direct survivor is also evaluated using a follow-up questionnaire distributed to both the survivor and the survivor's therapist (see Appendix C-2). If any clinically significant adverse emotional impact is detected by any of the tests or on the follow-up questionnaire, the offender-therapist contacts the survivor therapist to recommend that all survivor-offender communication and/or contact be stopped again and that the survivor begin immediate psychotherapy sessions to remediate the stress associated with the offender contact. After Intervention 8, the offender completes another offender-impact questionnaire. An outline of ERT Level 2 interventions appears on Table 1.

Not all direct or indirect survivors feel that the apology letters are sincere or helpful, and some decline to receive an apology from the offender. In order to decrease the stress associated with making the apology session decision, survivors are informed that if for any reason they choose not to participate in an apology session now, they retain the right to schedule a session at any time in the future. If the survivor declines an apology session, the offender must sign a behavior contract to apologize to the survivor if and when the survivor and her/his therapist decide to allow it. Although the offender may have been refused the opportunity to apologize by the survivor, they are not excused from their responsibility to demonstrate a prosocial, helpful behavior toward survivors. In this situation, the offender must conduct an Offender Information Group for survivors during which the offender reads their apology letter, apologizes for their behavior, and answers any questions the survivors ask.

For an Offender Information Group session to be held, arrangements are made with a local survivor treatment group for two or three offenders whose survivors chose not to meet with them to address the survivor therapy group. The members of the survivor group decide whether to meet with the offenders. A separately scheduled meeting for the session is held in order to give survivors the option of not attending without having to miss any of their regular group meetings. For the survivors, the purpose of the Offender Information Group is for them to be able to ask questions, express feelings, confront fears, and regain a sense of mastery and control over their lives.

---

12. With younger survivors, different anxiety and locus of control scales are selected which are more suited to their age group; the State-Trait Anxiety Inventory for Children (Spielberger, 1973) and the Locus of Control Scale For Children (Nowicki & Strickland, 1973).

13. The "state" anger measure taps anger at a particular time, while "trait" anger measures a person's general tendency toward experiencing anger. The trait anger measure has two subscales: angry temperament, a general tendency to experience and express anger without specific provocation; and angry reaction, a tendency to express anger when feeling criticized by others.

For the offenders, the purpose of the Offender Information Group is emotional restitution by demonstrating prosocial behavior towards survivors, taking full responsibility for their behavior, explaining to the best of their ability the chain of events and decisions that led up to their offending and answering any questions the survivors ask. In order to provide a positive peer participant model, an offender who has successfully apologized to their direct survivor is included in the Offender Information Group. As in the Survivor Impact Group, both offender- and survivor-therapists attend and sit between the survivors and offenders so that no survivor is sitting next to an offender. In addition, the Offender Information Group is held in the survivor treatment center and the video camera is again placed behind the survivors so that it focuses only on the offenders.

Prior to the Offender Information Group, information that the survivors want to know from the offenders is gathered using a one-page "Things I Want to Know" questionnaire (see Appendix C-3). Survivor and offender participants separately complete a State-Trait Anxiety Inventory and a State-Trait Anger Expression Inventory before and after the Offender Information Group. In addition, all survivors are asked to fill out a "Thoughts and Feelings Questionnaire" and all offenders complete an offender-impact questionnaire to tap the subjective impact of the group on its participants in other areas.

Case Studies and Clinical Evaluation Data

Single Case Study: All Interventions (1-8)

"Ron's" case was selected to illustrate the potential impact of the various interventions used in ERT. At the time of treatment, Ron was a 17-year-old minority male who molested his younger sister Tina, starting when she was 8 and continuing to age 11. Ron lived with his mother, mother's boyfriend, younger brother, and two sisters. Ron was a high school senior with good academic achievement (3.0 grade point average) and poor school conduct (truancy and school suspensions for fighting). Ron's psychological testing revealed above-average intelligence and an MMPI personality profile indicating social introversion along with problems with being assertive.

Ron admitted fondling Tina's vagina, performing cunnilingus on her, having her perform fellatio on him, simulating intercourse, and attempting vaginal inter- course on Tina. Ron was aware that Tina had been molested by his older brother in the past and he used her vulnerability, along with manipulation, games, and bribery, to get Tina to comply with his sexual abuse. Ron committed these offenses on Tina approximately three times a week for three years. Ron's responses on a questionnaire about his maladaptive cognitions were as follows:

Self-statements before each offense against Tina

1. "I really shouldn't do this, but it won't really hurt anybody."
2. "Mom's not home, it feels good, and I won't get caught."

Self-statements during his offenses

1. "This feels good."
2. "I shouldn't be doing this, but it's not hurting anybody."
3. "She said yes."

Self-statements after each offense

1. "I didn't force her to do anything."
2. "It wasn't rape, she said I could so it's OK."
3. "I won't get caught, and I'm not going to do this again."

Ron was finally caught, charged with sexual misconduct and required to complete treatment at the Youth Sex Offender program in Stark County, Ohio by the local Department of Human Services.

Although Ron continued to live in the home during the time that both he and his sister were in treatment, he was required to comply with strict survivor-safety standards, including: (1) 24-hour supervision by an adult who was aware of his offenses while around Tina; (2) a complete "hands-off" policy with Tina; (3) secure sleeping arrangements to ensure that Ron did not have undetected access to Tina at night; and (4) a "gag order" preventing Ron from discussing his sexual abuse or any sexual issue with Tina except in the presence of a mental health professional during a psychotherapy session.

After the Intervention 1 process of reading and discussing the newspaper articles on the types of thoughts and feelings that survivors experience, Ron completed his offender-impact questionnaire and homework assignment. Ron rated Intervention 1 as having a considerable impact (i.e., "quite a bit" or above) in 11 of 21 areas covered (52%) (see Table 2). His written comments on what affected him the most were about the article specifically describing the survivor trauma suffered and "the fact that the guy used violence against the lady."

Ron received a 75 percent grade on his Intervention 1 homework assignment. His responses to the assignment questions were characterized as follows:

1. How survivors think: self-blame.
2. How survivors feel: dirty, unwanted, and unattractive.
3. How the survivor's life was affected: stages of trauma lasting a lifetime.
4. His thoughts and feelings: anger toward the offender (in the articles) and sympathy for the survivor.
5. Was justice done: "I feel that no matter how old the crime is the person should be able to pay for it. The evidence in this case might be old but the emotional scars of the survivor are still fresh."
6. Were you ever a survivor and what feelings did these articles bring back:
   an affirmative response and feelings of anger towards the offender.[14]

After the Intervention 2 process of reading and discussing the teenage survivors' letters expressing their feelings about their offenders and the enabling parent, as well as the impact of sexual abuse on survivors in general, Ron completed his offender-impact questionnaire and his Intervention 2 homework assignment. Ron rated Intervention 2 as having a considerable impact on

---

14. Ron had been molested as a child and had been in treatment for those issues. Offenders who have histories as victims are referred for victim treatment only *after* they take full responsibility for their offense behavior and demonstrate prosocial behavior toward victims.

Table 2		
Areas of Impact on Ron After Each Intervention		
Intervention 1	**Intervention 2**	**Intervention 3**
1) survivor trauma 6) sorrow level 7) concern level 8) regret level 9) self-disgust level 10) guilt level 11) self-anger level 15) selfish behavior 18) no right to offend 20) responsibility 21) relapse avoidance	1) survivor trauma 2) role reversal 7) concern level 8) regret level 9) self-disgust level 10) guilt level 11) self-anger level 15) selfish behavior 16) damage done 17) thoughts of others 18) no right to offend 20) responsibility 21) relapse avoidance	1) survivor trauma 2) role reversal 3) emotional level 5) depression level 6) sorrow level 7) concern level 8) regret level 9) self-disgust level 10) guilt level 11) self-anger level 15) selfish behavior 16) damage done 17) thoughts of others 18) no right to offend 20) responsibility 21) relapse avoidance
Intervention 4	**Intervention 6**	**Intervention 8**
1) survivor trauma 3) emotional level 4) anxiety level 8) regret level 9) self-disgust level 10) guilt level 12) fear of facing 15) selfish behavior 16) damage done 17) thoughts of others 18) no right to offend 19) making excuses 20) responsibility 21) relapse avoidance	1) survivor trauma 2) role reversal 3) emotional level 4) anxiety level 5) depression level 6) sorrow level 7) concern level 8) regret level 9) self-disgust level 10) guilt level 11) self-anger level 12) fear of facing 15) selfish behavior 16) damage done 17) thoughts of others 18) no right to offend 19) making excuses 20) responsibility 21) relapse avoidance	1) survivor trauma 2) role reversal 3) emotional level 4) anxiety level 5) depression level 6) sorrow level 7) concern level 8) regret level 9) self-disgust level 10) guilt level 11) self-anger level 12) fear of facing 15) selfish behavior 16) damage done 17) thoughts of others 18) no right to offend 19) making excuses 20) responsibility 21) relapse avoidance
Note: Numbers indicate the questions on the "Learning Experience Questionnaire" (Appendix B-1) that Ron indicated had a considerable impact ("quite a bit" or above). Questions 13 (fear of reprisal) and 14 (control loss fear) were the only two areas that Ron did not indicate had a considerable impact at some point during ERT.		

him in 13 of 21 areas covered (62%) (see Table 2). His comments indicated that the two specific letters from the survivor to her offender and to her mother affected him the most.

Ron received an 84 percent grade on his Intervention 2 homework assignment. His responses to the assignment questions were characterized as follows:

1. List the initial effects of sexual abuse: anger, fear, loneliness, insecurity, and confusion.
2. Discuss survivor feelings: "She feels anger for what happened to her and the help she didn't get. She hates the feelings she's having, the person who did this to her and is confused as to why it happened to her."
3. Who the feelings are about: "The feelings are mostly about herself. The anger and hate is directed towards the offender."
4. Who the survivor is most angry with: "I think she is most angry with her stepdad who offended her."
5. The necessary steps for survivors to manage their trauma: "The survivors must get help and support from their families who are willing to talk about it and they must seek counseling. It would also help if the offender was punished."
6. When will the survivor adjust: "I don't know when she will adjust but it will be a long time."

After observing the emotionally intense videotape of four survivors describing the impact of the offenses committed against them, Ron's offender-impact questionnaire indicated that Intervention 3 had a considerable impact on him in 16 of 21 areas (76%). His comment on what affected him the most about the survivor videotape was "the tears in the one lady's eyes as she told about how her family must have known."

After attending the Survivor Impact Group in Intervention 4, Ron rated Intervention 4 as having a considerable impact on him in 14 areas (67%) (see Table 2). His comments on what affected him the most about the Survivor Impact Group were, "When (the survivors) asked how could someone do this and when they were talking about the way they felt."

In summary, all four Level 1 interventions had an impact on Ron in the areas of eliciting emotional responses of regret, self-disgust, and guilt. In addition, these interventions had a cognitive impact involving thoughts of the selfish, unjustified nature of his offense behavior, accepting responsibility for the offense behavior, and motivation to avoid relapse. However, only the Survivor Impact Session was able to raise Ron's level of anxiety about facing his deviant, criminal behavior and admitting that he was making excuses for his behavior. Since making excuses such as blaming the survivor, justifying, or minimizing the behavior and not experiencing anxiety about illegal/deviant behaviors are critical relapse components, the Survivor Impact Session was considered a necessary relapse prevention component for Ron.

During the fifth intervention, Ron said he felt that his mother, sister Michelle, and younger brother Dwayne had experienced a lot of emotional pain about his molesting of his sister Tina. Thus, these family members were defined as indirect survivors of his abuse. Ron discussed and revised his apology letter to his indirect survivors based on feedback from his offender group. Since some of Ron's family did not hold him completely responsible and his mother tended to blame the survivor, Ron's letter focused on these issues. Ron received an "A" from his group on the final draft of his indirect-survivor letter. Ron's therapist contacted Ron's mother several days after his letter was mailed. She indicated that she found his apology letter sincere and helpful.

Ron's therapist agreed with this opinion and, with Ron's mother's consent, scheduled an indirect-survivor apology session. Ron's apology letter to his indirect survivors appears in Table 3.

Table 3
Ron's Apology Letter to the Indirect Survivors
of his Sexual Abuse

Dear Mom, Michelle and Dwayne,

I'm writing this to say that I'm sorry for the terrible burden that I've placed upon our family by sexually abusing Tina. It's not her fault that I've created such a burden, but rather it's my fault. I should of shown Tina what's right, as her older brother, instead of showing her things that are wrong and harmful to her.

I understand that I've caused a lot of pain and it's important to work with me to show Tina that my actions are not her fault. The pain I've caused will hurt Tina forever, but we can help her by showing that things aren't her fault.

I know I let this family down and betrayed the trust that was placed in me. Through this betrayal of trust, I've created a tension between the relationship we have with Tina and with each other. This tension will never go away but will diminish hopefully as time goes on.

I accept full responsibility for what I've done and it's important that you fully accept that it is me who should receive all the blame, not Tina. Again, I'm sorry for the burden I've caused and that it's not Tina's fault for my actions.

Another thing, no one else in the family is at fault for my offense, I offended Tina on my own free will. I had no right to sexually abuse Tina but, I did and it's my fault.

Ron

In Intervention 6, a therapy session was scheduled for Ron to apologize to his mother, Michelle, and Dwayne for the damage he had done to Tina and to their family. After the apology session to his indirect survivors, Ron completed another offender-impact questionnaire while his mother completed an indirect survivor follow-up questionnaire.

Ron rated Intervention 6 as having a considerable impact on him in 19 of the 21 areas (90%) covered by the offender-impact questionnaire (see Table 2). Ron's comment on what affected him most about this learning experience was "When Dwayne (my brother) said that no matter what I do, he'd still love me and my mom and Michelle agreed."

On her follow-up questionnaire, Ron's mother indicated that both the apology letter and session had the same impact on her. Ron's mother indicated that receiving the apology letter and the apology in session helped her "a little" with: (1) accepting what happened; (2) being able to discuss the abuse; (3) being honest about her feelings; (4) feeling less guilty; (5) feeling less worried; (6) feeling less depressed; and (7) feeling less angry. Ron's mother said that she felt that the apology letter "prepares you for the apology session" and that the apology session "reinforced my knowledge of who is responsible." Ron's apology-session behavior was judged appropriate, sincere, and helpful by both his indirect survivors and his therapist. He was therefore allowed to write an apology letter to his direct survivor, Tina. The letter was then mailed to Tina's therapist.

At the time of treatment, Tina was an 11-year-old minority female who was the youngest of four children in her family. Tina was an above-average student in an advanced class of the fifth grade. Tina was first molested at about age 4 by Ron's older brother who no longer lives in the home. She was later molested by Ron for 3 years. She disclosed her abuse to a non-family member who reported it to the authorities. Ron's apology letter to Tina appears in Table 4.

Table 4
Ron's Apology Letter to the Survivor of his Sexual Abuse

Dear Tina,

I'm writing this to apologize for abusing you. I had no right to take advantage of you. As your older brother, I should have guided you along the right path and not have committed sexual abuse against you. But, out of selfishness I took you along the wrong path and did things to you that were wrong. It's not your fault that I did this. I was the older one and I knew it was wrong and I'm ashamed of my actions. As your brother, I should have taught you things that are right and not lead you into something that is wrong. What I did hurt you a lot and again, I apologize. You did nothing wrong, instead you did the right thing by telling on me. If you hadn't I wouldn't be getting help for my problem. Telling on me was the brave and right thing to do. I needed help and telling on me was the right thing to do.

I know that your having to leave the room when I come in with nobody else around[15] must make you feel that what I've done is your fault. Well it isn't your fault at all, it's my fault. From the start, nothing has been your fault and I'm sorry that you feel this way. The rule about us not being in a room together alone isn't meant to punish you but to protect you from me ever taking advantage of you again.

Ron

After receiving and discussing Ron's apology letter, Tina and her therapist completed separate follow-up questionnaires on the impact of the offender-apology letter. On each questionnaire, the first set of questions asked for responses in seven areas on a series of five-point rating scales. Tina's responses to "mark your opinion on how receiving the apology letter has helped or hurt you" on the rating scales were as follows: (1) it helped her between "a little more" and "much more" in terms of accepting what happened to her; (2) it left her "about the same" regarding being open to giving details of the abuse; (3) the apology letter helped her somewhat (i.e., between "about the same" and "a little more") with her honesty about her feelings; (4) the letter

---

15. Ron's behavior contract requires that he not be alone with Tina, not that she must leave the room when he enters it. This language was viewed as a difficulty Ron had in expressing the requirement, not necessarily as an accurate portrayal of his survivor-safety standards which prevent him from entering a room where Tina is alone.

had helped her *decrease* feeling guilty/blaming self, feeling afraid or anxious, feeling sad and depressed, and feeling angry or hostile (all items she marked between "a little less" and "much less").

Tina's response to the question asking her to list any other ways that receiving the apology letter affected her was, "It helped me to open my eyes and see that it was not my fault." Her response to the question asking her if she would recommend that other survivors be given the opportunity to receive offender-apology letters was, "Yes, because it could help them see what I saw."

Tina's therapist was a licensed, Ph.D.- level psychologist with five years' experience as the director of a survivor treatment program. Tina's therapist responded to the rating scales on the therapist questionnaire as follows: (1) receiving the apology letter decreased Tina's guilt/self-blame, fear and anxiety, and sadness/depression "a little"; (2) the apology letter left Tina "about the same" regarding her denial of what happened, being open to giving details of the abuse, and anger/hostility; and (3) the apology letter helped Tina's honesty about her feelings "a little."

Tina's therapist responded to the question asking him to list any other ways that receiving the apology letter affected Tina by writing, "It helps validate the client's movement toward exorcising herself of self-blame." His response to the question asking whether he would recommend that other survivors be given the opportunity to receive offender-apology letters was, "Yes. It provides the abused client with information needed to work through guilt/anger issues in a safe environment. It allows for assessment of the viability of face-to-face offender-survivor contact."

The feedback received after Intervention 7 from both Tina and her therapist on the impact of the apology letter was positive; therefore, Tina was asked if she would like Ron to apologize in person, and she said yes. At the time that both survivor and offender were brought together in treatment, Ron had been in a youth sex-offender treatment program receiving two hours of weekly group therapy and one hour of biweekly individual therapy for a period of one year. Ron had successfully completed the first level of ERT (i.e., all four interventions on survivor-impact understanding) before being allowed to communicate about his abuse to Tina. Tina had received one hour of weekly individual/family therapy for one year and was involved in a survivor- support group before the apology session. In addition, she received specific preparation for the apology session in her individual therapy where the format and expected content of the apology session was described. Tina was tested a week before the session was held and tested again immediately after the apology session.

At Tina's request, her therapist and her mother were present during the apology session with Ron and his therapist. Ron started by reading his letter to Tina.

He was visibly nervous and Tina fidgeted. During the session, Ron verbally accepted full responsibility for his offense behavior. He reinforced the fact that his behavior was not her fault and proclaimed his sincere apology and regret for the damage that his behavior had caused her. Tina said that she accepted Ron's apology and admitted her anger toward him. Although Tina knew she had permission to express herself in any manner that she wished, she chose not to vent her feelings during the session. Aft.er the apology session with Tina, Ron completed another offender-impact questionnaire, and Tina was retested. Aft.er Tina's testing both she and her therapist completed follow-up questionnaires.

On all four tests administered to Tina, lower scores indicate less intense symptoms. Tina's test scores before and after her apology session appear in Table 5.[16]

In summary, of the 8 test measures examined before and after Tina's apology session, 7 decreased and 1 stayed the same. Three of these changes were clinically relevant. Tina's level of depression decreased to zero. Her general tendency towards experiencing anger and her tendency to express anger without specific provocation had decreased from a clinically "elevated" level to "not elevated." The results of this testing indicate that there was no

Table 5 Tina's Test Scores		
	Pretest	Posttest
1. Beck Depression Inventory Score	8	0
2. State Anxiety T-Score	57	50
3. Trait Anxiety T-Score	50	43
4. State Anger T-Score	46	46
5. Trait Anger T-Score	74	66
6. Angry Temperament T-Score	80	55
7. Angry Reaction T-Score	67	60
8. Locus of Control Scale for Children Score	15	10

adverse emotional impact on Tina's level of anxiety or feeling externally controlled after her apology session with Ron. In addition, these results revealed a clinical improvement in Tina marked by a decrease in general feelings of depression and anger along with a decrease in unprovoked angry outbursts.

After the apology session and post-testing, Tina and her therapist completed separate follow-up questionnaires on the impact of the offender-apology session. On each questionnaire, the first set of questions required responses in seven areas on a series of five-point rating scales. Tina's responscs to "mark your opinion on how receiving the apology session has helped or hurt you" on the rating scales provided appear as follows: participating in the apology session helped her accept what happened to her, be open to giving details of the abuse, and be honest about her feelings "much more"; the apology session left her feeling "a little less" afraid or anxious; and she felt "much less" guilty/self-blaming, sad and depressed, and angry or hostile after her apology session.

Tina's response to the question asking her to list any other ways that participating in the apology session affected her was similar to her response to the apology letter: "It helped me to open up my feelings and feel like it wasn't my fault." Her response to the question asking her if she would recommend that other survivors be given the opportunity to receive offender-apology sessions was, "Sure, because it would help them admit what happened and to know that it wasn't their fault."

16. Interpretation of test scores is described in Appendix D for all tests except the Locus of Control Scale for Children. Scores in the range of 13 to 21 on the Locus of Control Scale for Children for female, fifth grade students can be considered within the normal range.

Tina's therapist responded to the rating scales on the therapist questionnaire as follows: after the apology session Tina's denial of what happened, openness to giving details of the abuse, along with her fear and anxiety decreased "a little"; the apology session increased Tina's honesty about her feelings and anger/hostility "a little"; and her level of guilt/self-blame and sadness/depression was reported as "much less" after the apology session.

Tina's therapist did not give a specific response to the question asking him to list any other ways that receiving the apology letter affected Tina. His response to the question asking if he would recommend that other survivors be given the opportunity to receive offender-apology sessions was, "Yes-it would appear to facilitate the survivor in getting over the hump of self-blame."

Ron rated Intervention 8 as having a considerable impact on him in the same 19 offender-impact questionnaire areas (90%) that he reported in the sixth intervention after his apology to his indirect survivors (see Table 2). Ron's comment on what affected him most about this intervention was, "When I had to apologize."

In summary, the subjective reports of Tina and her therapist on their impact questionnaires supported the results of her testing before and after the apology session. Both sources of data indicated that Tina had received some apparent benefits from the session and revealed no clinically significant adverse emotional effects. Based on their experience with the apology session, both Tina and her therapist recommended that other survivors be offered the opportunity to receive offender-apology sessions. Ron's two apology sessions had similar impacts on him, indicating that the indirect-survivor apology session was a good training session prior to apologizing to his actual survivor. The differences in the reports from the survivor and the therapist on levels of anger after the direct-survivor apology session reinforce the importance of including an objective anger measure in Intervention 8.

Clinical Evaluation Data:
Impact of Level 1 Interventions (1-4) on Offenders

During the same time period that Ron was in treatment, 14 male adolescents (13 Caucasian, 1 minority) ages 15-19 ($M = 16.8$) in two treatment groups received the four survivor-understanding interventions in Level 1 of ERT. Their offenses ranged from indecent exposure to forced intercourse rape and included same-gender as well as opposite-gender child molestations.

Since one goal of ERT Level 1 is to avoid the overwhelming emotional stress that may inhibit prosocial behavior, it is important to demonstrate that the interventions are set up in a hierarchy of perceived emotional impact by the offenders. A total impact score was computed on each offender after each intervention by adding up the response scores on each of the 21 5-point scales on the offender-impact questionnaire (Appendix B-1). In order to compare the overall impact of all four Level 1 interventions, the total impact scores of all offenders during each intervention were averaged together.

When all four mean (average) offender-impact questionnaire scores were ranked, as predicted they were in the same order as the interventions: the survivor newspaper articles produced the lowest total impact score on the offenders, followed by the survivor letters and the survivor videotape, with the Survivor Impact Session producing the greatest offender impact. The increase in impact across interventions in the predicted hierarchy direction was statisti-cally significant, indicating that there was a very high probability that these clinical evaluation findings were not accidental or due to chance.[17] The offenders' impact ratings supported the contention that the series of survivor-understanding interventions (i.e., ERT Level 1) are a hierarchy which gradually exposes offenders to increasing degrees of survivor impact.

Questions on the offender-impact questionnaire that revealed statistically significant differences in the impact of the four Level 1 interventions were further examined. This examination revealed that the Survivor Impact Session produced the largest number of statistically significant impact questions over the survivor newspaper articles, followed by the survivor letters, and finally, the survivor videotape.[18] This finding also supports the contention that Level 1 of ERT is a hierarchy of interventions.

During the (videotaped) Survivor Impact Session, no offender made inappropriate comments or nonverbal gestures. One offender made an inappropriate comment about the survivors on the offender-impact questionnaire distributed after the session. That offender wrote, "I wish I could date the three" survivors; as a consequence, he was not allowed to go on to Level 2 where he would face his direct and indirect survivor(s). That offender was later terminated from outpatient treatment and referred for residential treatment.

The results of this clinical evaluation indicated that having several adolescent survivors of sexual abuse explain their trauma directly to a group of adolescent sex offenders produced the greatest impact on the offenders as measured by: (1) the total score of all 21 of the impact questions that offenders were asked to rate; and (2) the number of questions on which offenders rated the Survivor Impact Session as highest in impact on them. In addition, the offender ratings also revealed that having adolescent sex abuse survivors explain their trauma to a group of adolescent sex offenders produced a greater impact than any other intervention on how much the offender perceived his offense as being unjustified, regardless of his past cognitions or affect. This is considered important as it directly relates to the offender problem of rationalizing, justifying, or minimizing the effects they have on others.

After completing Level 1 of Emotional Restitution Training, all 14 offenders were required to write indirect-survivor apology letters. One offender stated that he was not ready to mail the letter, giving the group as a whole a 93 percent rate of prosocial behavior compliance. Although offender ratings indicated that the survivor impact group had the greatest effect on them, subjective comments by the offenders indicate that they benefited from all of the interventions. Furthermore, it is believed that the sequence of the four learning experiences was beneficial in the development of emotional restitution (the apology letter). Although the effect of putting the offenders through a survivor-understanding hierarchy produced a positive emotional and cognitive effect-particularly where the Survivor Impact Session was concerned-the Survivor Impact Sessions could not be continued if they helped the offender at the emotional expense of the survivor

---

17. "Repeated measures ANOVA $F_{(3,39)}= 3.51$, $p<.05$. For further statistical results see Yokley (1989).

18. Post hoc comparisons were conducted using paired comparison t-tests at the .01 level of significance. For a more complete description see Yokley (1989).

volunteers. The psychological test results on the amount and type of stress experienced by the survivors who conducted the impact group that Ron attended are provided in the following group case study.

Group Case Study:
Survivors during Intervention 4 (the Survivor Impact Group)

When Ron went through Intervention 4, five female survivors (4 Caucasian, 1 Minority), aged 18, 17, 17, 13 and 11, who were in treatment at a sexual abuse survivor treatment program, volunteered to participate in the ERT Survivor Impact Group. These volunteers were asked to complete the Beck Depression Inventory, the State-Trait Anxiety Inventory, and the Rotter Internal-External Locus of Control Scale to measure their levels of depression, anxiety, and helplessness. The survivors took these tests one week before and one week after the impact session. They also completed a "Thoughts and Feelings Questionnaire" after participating in the Survivor Impact Group (see Appendix B-3).

The three oldest of the five survivor volunteers attended the impact session and served as panelists. Two of the three were incest survivors and one was a rape survivor. Each panelist informed the offender group exactly what happened to her and how being sexually victimized affected her life. The survivors then confronted the offenders with questions focusing on the issue of why the offenders committed their crimes. Offenders who had been victimized in the past were of particular interest to the survivor panelists who wondered how someone who had been a survivor could in turn abuse another person.

On all three test measures administered, lower scores indicate less intense symptoms. All three survivors' post-session Beck Depression Inventory scores (taken one week after the Survivor Impact Session) stayed about the same and were within two points of their pre-session scores. Survivor State Anxiety and Trait Anxiety remained at about the same level (i.e., an average increase of 2.3 and 1.7 points per survivor respectively). All three survivors' posttest scores on the Locus of Control Scale stayed about the same (within two points of their pretest scores). The actual survivor test scores before and after the Survivor Impact Group appear in Appendix D.

In summary, of the 12 depression, anxiety, and locus of control test measures on cognitive/affective state of the survivors who conducted the impact session (4 measures on 3 survivors), 2 went down (2 points or more), 9 stayed the same (within 2 points), and 1 went up (2 points or more). None of these changes was clinically significant, i.e., no change was so pronounced that symptoms had moved up or down between "elevated" and "not elevated." The absence of any clinically relevant increases on the test measures tends to indicate that there was no adverse emotional impact on the survivor volunteers' level of depression, anxiety, or feeling externally controlled during the period when the Survivor Impact Group was conducted.

When pretest scores were compared on survivors who attended and faced the offenders and those who did not attend, survivors who attended had lower average scores on both depression and anxiety, a finding that may be clinically relevant. Those who attended were also considerably older. Thus, some self-selection may have taken place with the younger, more depressed and anxious survivors electing not to attend. Specifically, the results of the present case study revealed that survivors under age 14 with Beck Depression Scores over 5, State Anxiety Scores over 49, and Trait Anxiety Scores over 46 did not attend the survivor impact group that they had volunteered to conduct. While this finding should not be used as absolute cut-off criteria for survivor volunteer selection, they suggest initial clinical guidelines of offering Survivor Impact Group participation to survivors who are older and exhibit fewer or less severe symptoms of depression and anxiety, until research studies provide empirically validated selection criteria. Average survivor test scores on survivors who attended and conducted the impact group, compared to the scores of those who did not attend, appear in Appendix D.

The comments below were recorded by the three survivor volunteers on the "Thoughts and Feelings Questionnaire" after they conducted the impact group and immediately following their psychological post-testing. In response to the question, "Please describe how coming face-to-face and speaking with or confronting the sex offenders has helped or hurt you," the oldest survivor wrote, "It made me realize that often the offender themselves have been hurt so in turn they hurt others. Before, I imagined that they'd be worse but now they are just everyday people that you could meet in school." The second survivor recorded, "It has helped me to understand why someone would do something that would hurt another person." The third survivor wrote, "This has helped me because I got a chance to see and hear why these types of people do what they do. Although nothing they did is or ever will be justified, I can somewhat understand them and their actions. Also, since I talked to them and asked them questions, I feel maybe I can talk to my offender and ask him the same questions." This survivor went on to write, "I don't feel as angry about what happened to me or toward my offender, because I had a chance to hear some explanations of why the offense happened. Many guys were abused as a child, and I can sympathize with that fact. What they did is not justified, but I can understand them, and think maybe something like this has happened to my offender."

The comments below are the survivor panelists' responses to the question, "Would you recommend that other survivors be given the opportunity to confront offend- ers or speak to them face-to-face? Why?" Mary, the oldest panelist, responded, "Yes. It may help them to deal with their hostility and to possibly get some answers." The second survivor responded, "Yes. I think the offender should hear what survivors go through to make them realize what they've done. It is also good for a survivor because they get to ask them questions and better understand how things like that could happen." The third survivor responded, "Yes, but only if they are sure they can handle the situation. This gives you a chance to find out what these people feel and think about what they did. It may give the survivor an idea of how their offender feels. Also, you can express your feelings of anger without directing it toward anyone in particular." After they completed their' posttests and questionnaires, the survivors were given the offenders' written reactions to the impact session (see Appendix E).

That same week in a therapy session, the third survivor's therapist gave her a written homework assignment to "describe the impact of the offender's statements on yourself after reading their description of how they were affected by your presentation." That survivor wrote the following response:

I feel good about what I did. Talking to these guys helped them in ways no psychologist or counselor could ever help. I am glad to see my points were taken into consideration. What I said to them made them think a lot and taught them a lot which makes me feel good. Knowing that I could help them just a little and knowing that they feel strongly about some things (such as "this will never go away" and "it will affect me the rest of my life") tells me that they do have feelings and they do feel bad about what happened to their survivors. Maybe they will put the survivor's feelings and what they are going through first, before what they themselves are going through, and realize the survivor is much worse off. This has also helped me in the area dealing with my own offender. Maybe he feels the same way these guys do, or maybe if I tell him what he did to me as a person, he'll feel this way, and maybe help him, or make him feel as bad as I did.

Nine months after the Survivor Impact Session, the second survivor's therapist gave her a written homework assignment to answer the question, "What kind of an effect do you think talking and listening to the sex offenders has had on you?" That survivor wrote, "It helped me to understand a little bit of why they do it. I was shocked to know that there are young kids doing it too. It also gave me relief because I got the chance to tell a sex offender what a survivor goes through when he doesn't even think it matters to the person."

In summary, the subjective reports of the survivor panelists on the impact questionnaire revealed that all three found the Survivor Impact Group helpful in some manner and recommended that other survivors be offered the opportunity to confront or speak to offenders. These subjective survivor reports supported the results of the survivor testing before and after exposure to the offenders in indicating no clinically significant adverse emotional effects on the survivor volunteers. However, since there were too few survivor volunteers (n=3) in this clinical evaluation to conduct a conclusive statistical analysis, caution must be exercised in generalizing the test results to other survivors.

In a final word of caution, remember that ERT involves survivors in impact groups only with youth sex offenders who have successfully completed both the first two TASC treatment components during some 8-to-12 months of treatment *and* the first three ERT survivor-understanding interventions. In addition, none of the survivor volunteers exhibited signs of clinical depression or anxiety on the test measures employed and only one survivor volunteer showed clinical signs of feeling externally controlled. The effect of offender interactions with survivors who exhibit clinical signs of depression or anxiety or survivor interactions with offenders who were not prepared in the manner outlined above is unknown. The participation of survivors in apology sessions or other survivor-offender interactions where the survivor emotional state or offender preparation is in question could lead to an adverse emotional impact.

Group Case Study:
Offenders in Intervention 8 (Offender Information Group)

Due to his progress in treatment, Ron was asked to assist two offenders in his program with their Offender Information Group. The two offenders with Ron were 18- and 19-year-old white males who had completed Level 1 of ERT and had written responsible and appropriate apology letters. One offender's apology session was declined by his indirect survivor (the mother of the child he molested),[19] and the other of- fender was unable to apologize because his survivor had moved and could not be located.

The survivors present were five white females aged 19, 16, 15, 15, and 14 who had been in psychotherapy for 24 months, 6 months, 12 months, 13 months, and 24 months, respectively. The "Things I want to know" questionnaires from the survivors in this group contained the following questions for the offenders:

- Why did he go after me when he had mom?
- Why did this guy that I don't even know, choose me (What did I do to deserve to be chosen)?
- Why choose a young person with no idea of what's going on, why not choose someone their own age?
- Why choose that person?
- Do you shy away from females now?
- Are you scared that you may offend again?
- Why did you do what you did to me?
- Why did you choose me instead of someone else on the street?
- Why did it have to be me, why did you do what you did?
- Could you have stopped if you had wanted to?
- What was the real reason you did this?

The three offenders were introduced by their therapist, who then reviewed the purpose of the session. Each offender disclosed his offense history, why he was in treatment, what he believed led to his offense behavior, and the maladaptive cognitions and faulty attributions that allowed him to continue offending. The first offender then told the group that he wanted to apologize to the mother of his survivor, "but my selfish stupidity took everything away, and she cannot see me right now because of all of the pain that I put her through. So I'm signing a contract that says if at any time in my life, she wants to see me and hear me say that I am sorry, I'll be there. It's not something that I am doing because I'm forced to or have to, I'm doing this because I want to." The second offender explained that his past survivors lived out of state and his most recent survivor could not be located.

Both offenders then read their apology letters to the group. During the discussion that followed, several survivors said they wished their offenders had apologized. One of the survivors told of how her offender denied everything, and one of the offenders responded, "I know that some of you will never hear your offender say that they're sorry, because they think they can get out of it, or they're scared to. But I'm sorry for what those people did to you. I hope someday that they'll realize what they did wrong." That offender went on to describe his four-month period of denial, what his excuse was, how he initially minimized the impact of his behavior, then told some-but not all-of the story, and gradually learned to accept responsibility for his crime. The survivors

---

19. The reason that the survivor's mother gave for declining the apology session did not involve any complaints from her about the content of the apology letter but was because she indicated that she was still too upset about the offense to speak with the offender.

then asked questions regarding offense behavior and offenders. During the group, all three offenders held each other accountable for their offense· behavior by providing each other with feedback on a couple of occasions when language was used that did not take full responsibility. On one occasion, an offender corrected himself.

The results of the survivor testing before and after the Offender Information Group revealed the following (lower scores indicate less intense affect): scores for both State and Trait Anxiety remained at about the same level (an average increase of 2.4 and .2 points per survivor respectively); scores for State and Trait Anger, Angry Temperament, and Angry Reaction remained about the same (an average decrease of 1.0, 2.4, 2.4 points per survivor for the first three survivors, and an average increase for the fourth survivor of 1.4 points). In summary, of the 30 anger and anxiety test measures on the survivors who attended the Offender Information Group session, 24 of the posttest scores (80%) were about the same (within 2 points) or lower than the pretest scores. The actual survivor test scores before and after the Offender Information Group appear in Appendix F.

The results of Ron's testing before and after he participated in conducting the Offender Information Group revealed a clinically relevant *decrease* in State and Trait Anxiety along with a decrease in state anger. Ron's other three measures of anger all remained about the same. One offender with Ron had a clinically relevant *increase* in state anger and anxiety after the group. When asked about the anger increase this offender stated that he became angry when hearing about the survivors being assaulted. When asked to explain, he said that he was angry at "the people molesting and raping" the survivors who had spoken to him in the group. He went on to explain, "It made me mad that there's people like me out there. It's kind of stupid, I can't control what those people do, it's just that they're out there hurting others. I'm angry at myself for doing it also." This offender's anger increase during the group was considered an indicator of positive therapeutic change. A summary of offender test scores appears in Appendix F.

None of the changes in the test levels of *survivor* anxiety or anger reached a level considered clinically relevant (i.e., indicated that symptoms had moved up or down between "elevated" and "not elevated"). The absence of any clinically relevant increases on the survivor test measures taken tend to indicate that there was no adverse emotional impact on the survivor's level of anxiety or anger as a result of participating in the Offender Information Group. However, it should be noted that during the Offender Information Group, one survivor cried, did not talk and exhibited an increase in state anxiety which approached clinical relevance on her post-group testing. When contacted, her therapist disclosed that like the offenders, this survivor was also involved in delinquent behaviors. In her therapist's opinion, seeing some of her behaviors in the offenders may have increased her anxiety. In addition, this survivor had disclosed three past suicide attempts over the past six months and had never cried before. Her therapist viewed the tears shed during the group as a therapeutic breakthrough. The fact that this survivor was the youngest in the group (age 14), exhibited symptoms of depression (withdrawal and crying), and was the only one with a State Anxiety pretest score over 49 supports the results found in the Survivor Impact

Group: younger survivors who express more feelings of depression and anxiety may not be appropriate candidates for survivor-offender interactions.[20]

The comments below were recorded by the five survivors on their "Thoughts and Feelings Questionnaires" after they participated in the Offender Information Group and immediately following their psychological post-testing. In response to the question, "Please describe how coming face-to-face and speaking with or confronting the sex offenders has helped or hurt you," Mary, the oldest survivor, simply wrote, "It has helped." The second survivor responded, "It's helped a tremendous amount. You can tell they take the blame. It is so weird, I never thought in any time of their life that they would care or even want to care to try to understand what we went through. I guess they really are human. They can be helped. I feel for [the offender who had been molested]." The third survivor wrote, "It has helped me to understand somewhat. They really explained a lot of different things and that really helped me understand more." The fourth survivor responded, "It has helped me. I can maybe figure out why he did this to me. Thank You." The last and youngest survivor wrote, "It helped me to know some guys can admit it. It hurt me 'cause it brought back all my feelings against sex offenders."

The comments below are the survivors' responses to the question, "Would you recommend that other survivors be given the opportunity to confront offenders or speak to them face-to-face? Why?" Mary responded, "Yes. You're able to express your thoughts openly without fear." The second survivor wrote, "Definitely, it helps so much, you can't ignore it when they're there in your face, you feel the honesty and shame." The third survivor responded, "Yes, if they feel they could. So then the survivor's feelings are out in the open to them. It may help both ways." The fourth survivor wrote, "Yes. Maybe it could help them too." The youngest survivor responded, "Yes, so they know how we feel too."

Ron's offender-impact questionnaire indicated that the Offender Information Group had a considerable impact on Ron in all areas measured except two (feeling general sadness and fear of reprisal). This result was similar to the impact Ron experienced after the sixth and eighth intervention apology sessions. The two offenders with Ron recorded a similar impact on their questionnaires, but of a higher magnitude, on all measures. Ron's comment on what affected him most about this learning experience was, "When the two girls on the right began to cry a little, I felt sorry for what had happened to them." The other two offenders responded to the same question with, "How the survivors were violated" and "Knowing how the survivor really feels. I'm mad at myself and all of the other offenders."

In summary, the subjective reports of the *survivors* on the impact questionnaire after the Offender Information Group revealed positive results similar to those found after the Survivor Impact Group. Specifically, all five survivors indicated that they found the Offender Information Group helpful in some manner and recommended that other survivors be offered the opportunity to

---

20. Although a pattern may be developing here, these case study results should not be used as absolute cut-off criteria for survivors to participate in survivor-offender interactions. Until research studies provide empirically validated selection criteria, sound clinical practice would recommend participation by older survivors who express fewer or less severe symptoms of depression and anxiety.

confront or speak to offenders. These subjective survivor reports supported the results of the survivors' testing before and after the Offender Information Group which revealed no clinically relevant adverse emotional effects on the survivor participants.

The psychological testing on the *offenders* before and after the Offender In- formation Group session revealed a decrease in anxiety but an increase in anger (primarily attributable to the offender who became very angry at himself and other offenders for their behavior after hearing the survivors discuss their trauma). The subjective offender reports revealed that conducting the Offender Information Group session had a strong affective impact. Since there were too few offenders (n = 3) in this clinical evaluation to conduct a conclusive statistical analysis, caution must be exercised in generalizing the test results to other offenders, particularly those who have not received 8 to 12 months of offender-specific treatment and specific survivor responsibility training.

Summary and Research Recommendations

The clinical evaluations data presented indicated that having several adolescent survivors of sexual abuse express their trauma directly to a group of adolescent sex offenders produced a greater impact on the offenders than any of the other survivor-understanding interventions utilized. All of the survivors who conducted the Survivor Impact Group or participated in the Offender Information Group indicated that they found these forms of survivor-offender interaction helpful in some manner and recommended that other survivors be offered the opportunity to confront or speak to offenders. The psychological testing before and after their participation in these groups revealed no clinically significant adverse emotional effects on the survivors. The single-case study data on the survivor apology session revealed no clinically significant adverse emotional effects on the survivor and some apparent benefits.

A number of case study findings in this report are clinically relevant and deserve research attention. First of all, the case study data revealed *no adverse impact on survivors* participating in three types of therapeutic survivor-offender interactions: the Survivor Impact Group, the offender-survivor apology session, and the Offender Information Group. These observations, however, must be interpreted with three important qualifications:(1) offenders were prepared by 8-12 months of treatment (focusing on honesty, accepting responsibility for the offense, and understanding their offense behavior pattern along with contributing fac- tors); (2) offenders completed ERT Level 1 training (survivor understanding) before their interactions with survivors; and (3) younger, more depressed and anxious survivors did not attend the Survivor Impact Group session in this clinical evaluation, and survivor-offender sessions could be contraindicated for them. Since offenders frequently have problems with lying and the present clinical evaluation includes self-report data, the emphasis on honesty and accurate self-reporting (qualification **#1**) cannot be overstated. During the first 8-12 months of TASC treatment accurate self-reporting is reinforced as the primary means of establishing dignity, self-respect, and social acceptance in the group. Offenders work toward the goal of being able to state, "You can call me a sex offender but you can't call me a liar."

With respect to the issue of selecting the best preparation approach for offenders' therapeutic interaction with survivors, the results of the clinical evaluation data on the impact of ERT Level 1 supports the contention that the Level **1** treatment process is an actual hierarchy of interventions ranked in order of increasing impact on the offender. This finding is important because if the offender's lack of appropriate cognitions and affect towards their survivors represents an affective avoidance response, as suggested, then arranging interventions in a hierarchy where offenders are gradually exposed to the anxiety/guilt-eliciting interventions should decrease their avoidance attempts. Offender attempts to avoid aversive affect include both behavioral responses (e.g., absence from treatment or late arrival at treatment group meetings) and cognitive responses (dysfunctional cognitions or thinking errors) that effectively discount or minimize personal responsibility. Decreasing the probabil-ity of avoidance responses by using a graded approach hierarchy to the feared stimulus (i.e., exposure *in vivo*) has sound theoretical support in the research literature (Marks, 1977). If future research supports these clinical evaluation results, then this intervention method may become the treatment approach of choice for the development of offender understanding and responsibility for survivor trauma.

While these results indicate that it is possible to construct a hierarchy of interventions followed by some promising prosocial behavior results, a cause-and-effect relationship has not been established. Future research needs to focus on establishing the link between Level 1 survivor-impact-understanding interventions and Level 2 prosocial *cognitive* change as well as *behavioral performance.*

Another offender preparation issue involves the importance of direct, specific feed- back on survivor trauma regardless of whether that feedback is administered via bibliotherapy prompts (from survivor letters) or *in vivo* (directly from the survivors). Intervention 2 case study comments indicated that letters from survivors that expressed their specific thoughts/feelings directly toward those who have affected them had more of an impact than a survivor letter which described the general effects of sexual abuse. However, since offenders tend to use maladaptive self-statements to justify why treatment issues do not apply to them (e.g., "This letter was written specifically to someone else not me, so my survivor may not have been hurt like that"), the general letter targeting all offenders should probably be included along with the specific letters. In addition, the case study data from Intervention 4 indicated that the direct feedback provided by survivors during the Survivor Impact Group had an impact on more variables associated with relapse prevention. These offender preparation observations need to be examined further under controlled research conditions.

Previous youth sex-offender programs have recommended the use of high quality dramatic television programs on the impact of sexual abuse (e.g., Cagney and Lacey, "Date Rape", CBS-TV air date 1/5/88) to promote offender understanding of survivors and to develop offenders' empathy (Ross and Loss, 1988); such programs have a strong appeal to the youth audience. Future research should determine whether the dramatic storyline of high quality sexual abuse television programs increases the impact of the information on the offender or triggers maladaptive self-statements which discount the feedback being given (e.g., "This is not real, I didn't hurt anyone as bad as those actors make it seem"). Certain types of offenders may respond best to the abuse impact information when it is set in a dramatic storyline presented by professional actors, while others may be more affected by videotapes of real survivors. Until there is some research data on this issue, mental health professionals utilizing videotapes to promote survivor understanding may want to include both types of presentations.

A final offender preparation issue is brought to light by the Intervention 6 and 8 case study observations which revealed a similar offender impact between the indirect- and direct-survivor apology sessions. Given that stimulus generalization is a function of how similar the target situation is to the training situation (Kazdin, 1975), the offender perception that the indirect-survivor apology session is in many ways similar to the apology session with the actual survivor is important. This perceived similarity means that the appropriate survivor interaction behaviors learned through behavior rehearsal (role playing, modeling, and receiving performance feedback) and practiced in the indirect-survivor apology session should generalize to the actual survivor apology session, improving offender performance in that session. While this approach currently has sound theoretical support, future research should compare the performance of offenders who conduct an indirect-survivor apology session as a practice procedure *after* behavior rehearsal with the performance of those who use behavior rehearsal as the only prior training technique to the apology session with the actual survivor to determine if the indirect-survivor session significantly improves offender performance in the direct-survivor session.

Although the application of the clinical evaluation model to three therapeutic survivor- offender interactions revealed no adverse impact on the survivors and offenders observed, the question of whether these interactions help or hurt the survivor or offender will remain a value- laden, emotionally charged issue until such time that these procedures are studied under carefully controlled research conditions. As the research questions raised above begin to be answered, the efficacy of ERT when applied to other survivor crimes such as domestic violence, drunk driving deaths, armed robbery, or premeditated murder will need to be examined.

References

Beck, A., & Steer, R. (1987). *Beck depression inventory manual.* New York: The Psychological Corporation, Harcourt Brace Jovanovich.

"Date Rape." (1988, January 5). *Cagney and Lacey.* New York: Columbia Broadcasting System.

Elliott, **R.,** Reimschuessel, C., Cislo, D., & Sack, N. (1985). Significant events and the analysis of immediate therapeutic impacts. *Psycho- therapy, 22,* 620-630.

Emmelkamp, P. (1982). In vivo treatments of agora- phobia. In A. Goldstein & D. Chamberless (Eds.), *Agoraphobia: Multiple perspectives on theory and treatment.* (pp. 43-75) New York: Wiley.

Hope and recovery: A twelve step guide for healing from compulsive sexual behavior. (1987). Minneapolis, MN: CompCare Publishers.

Kazdin, A. (1975). *Behavior modification in applied settings.* Homewood, IL: The Dorsey Press.

Knopp, F. H. (1982). *Remedial intervention in adolescent sex offenses: Nine program descriptions.* Orwell, VT: The Safer Society Press.

Knopp, F. H. (1984). *Retraining adult sex offenders: Methods and models.* Orwell, VT: The Safer Society Press.

Lord, J. (1989). *Victim impact panels: A creative sentencing approach.* Hurst, TX: Mothers Against Drunk Driving.

Marks, I. (1977). Phobias and obsessions. In J. Maser & M. Seligman (Eds.), *Experimental psycho- pathology.* (pp. 1 74-213) New York: Wiley.

Michelson, M. (1985). Flooding. In A. Bellak & M. Herson (Eds.), *Dictionary of behavior therapy techniques.* (pp. 126-130) New York: Pergamon Press.

"News of rape often revives victims' terror, guilt feelings." (1988, September 4). *Beacon Journal,* Akron, OH (pp. Cl, C2).

Nowicki, S., & Strickland, B. (1973). A locus of control scale for children. *Journal of Consulting and Clinical Psychology, 40(1),* 148-154.

Palmer, R. (1989, April). *Empathy: Frankly my dear, I don't give a damn.* Paper presented at the conference of the Ohio Coalition for the Treatment of Adolescent Sex Offenders, Co- lumbus, OH.

Pollak, M. (Field Producer). (1990). "Face to face" in *The reporters* [Film]. Beverly Hills, CA: STF Productions, Inc.

Riecken, H., & Boruch, R. (1974). *Social experimentation: A method for planning and evaluating social intervention.* New York: Academic Press.

Ross, J., & Loss, P. (1988). *Psychoeducational curriculum for the adolescent sex offender.* Un- published manuscript. Ross, Loss & Associates, P.O. Box 666, Mystic, CT 06355.

Rotter, J. (1966). Generalized expectancies for internal versus external control of reinforcement. *Psychological Monographs: General and Ap- plied, 80(1),* 1-28.

Sgroi, S. (1982). *Handbook of clinical intervention in child sexual abuse.* Lexington, MA: Lexington Books.

Spielberger, C. (1973). *STAIC preliminary manual for the state-trait anxiety inventory for children.* Palo Alto, CA: Consulting Psychologists Press.

Spielberger, C. (1983). *Manual for the state-trait anxiety inventory.* Palo Alto, CA: Consulting Psychologists Press.

Spielberger, C. (1988). *Manual for the state-trait anger expression inventory.* Odessa, FL: Psychological Assessment Resources.

"Stark rape victim anguishes over prosecution loop- hole." (1988, September 4). *Beacon Journal,* Akron, OH (pp. Al, A4).

Surviving Sexual Abuse [Videotape] (1987). Show- place Studio Productions (Producer). Berkeley, CA: University of California Extension Media Center.

Yokley, J.M. (1989, April). *An evaluation of four procedures used to develop victim empathy in youth sex offenders.* Paper presented at the conference of the Ohio Coalition for the Treatment of Adolescent Sex Offenders, Co- lumbus, OH.

APPENDICES

Appendix A   Therapist Letter to Indirect Survivor

Appendix B-1   Learning Experience Questionnaire (Offender Impact Questionnaire). Administered after interventions 1, 2, 3, 4, 6, and 8.

Appendix B-2   Behavior Contract for Survivor Impact Session (Intervention 4)

Appendix B-3   Thoughts and Feelings Questionnaire (Intervention 4, follow-up questionnaire for survivors who conduct impact group)

Appendix C-1   Parent/Guardian Questionnaire (Intervention 6, indirect survivor follow-up questionnaire)

Appendix C-2   Client Questionnaire (apology session) and Therapist or Survivor Advocate Questionnaire (apology session); (Intervention 8, survivor apology session, follow-up questionnaires on the impact of the offender apology session on the survivor)

Appendix C-3   Things I Want to Know (Intervention 8, Offender Information Group, questionnaire on information that the survivors want to know from the offenders)

Appendix D   Survivors' Psychological Test Scores Before and After the Survivor Impact Group

Appendix E   Offender Responses to the Survivor Impact Group

Appendix F   Survivor and Offender Psychological Test Scores Before and After the Offender Information Group

Appendix A
THERAPIST LETTER TO INDIRECT SURVIVOR

To: _____   Date: _____

Dear _____

We are contacting you at this time to share some very personal information with you concerning the past abuse of your child. The individual who offended against your child has been in treatment at our Youth Sex Offender Program for some time now. One part of our program treatment is a requirement that the offender take full responsibility for what he has done to your child and to you. Most offenders have made threats or statements which kept their survivor silent and which later act to interfere with their progress in therapy. Since we feel that the offender has the responsibility to make restitution, or in some way attempt to help the people he has hurt, we require at a minimum that our offenders offer you and your child an apology. This apology must take full responsibility for the offense and encourage your child to tell their therapist everything that is needed to help in treatment.

Although we generally view offender apologies as helpful in the treatment of survivors, in order to protect your child from any further emotional harm, we will not allow an apology session with your child unless: (1) both you and your child's therapist feel it would be helpful; and (2) the offender shows both you and your child's therapist that he can handle an apology session in a helpful manner. In order to demonstrate that he can handle himself in a helpful manner, we require that the offender convince you and your child's therapist that he can be helpful by: (1) writing an apology letter to you which you and your child's therapist consider to be appropriate; (2) apologizing to you in a session which both you and your child's therapist consider to be helpful; and (3) writing an appropriate apology letter to your child to be sent to your child's therapist and discussed with you and your child in a therapy session.

If, at any time in this process, you or your child's therapist do not feel that the offender's apology will be helpful to your child, you may immediately stop the process, and no apology to your child will take place.

Attached is a letter to you written by the offender as a first step toward taking full responsibility and making some effort toward emotional restitution for the offense. Also enclosed are some answers to questions about Youth Sex Offenders which are commonly asked by parents. You are under no obligation to read this letter. It is simply an offer made by our program which you may choose to accept. If you decide to read the apology letter, we hope that you will call your child's therapist and discuss arranging a meeting where the offender can apologize directly to you.

Sincerely,

_____   Telephone # _____

99

Appendix B-1
LEARNING EXPERIENCE QUESTIONNAIRE

Name:_____ Date:_____

Please mark any changes in your feelings or thoughts that you have had since your survivor
__News Articles; __Letters; __ Videotape; __Impact Session learning experience.

1. How much did you learn about survivor thoughts and feelings from this experience?

    |-------------------------|---------------------|---------------------|---------------------|

    Nothing   A Little   A Moderate Amount   Quite A Bit   A Great Deal

2. How much did this learning experience get you in touch with how you would feel if you were victimized or revictimized?

    |---------------------|---------------------|---------------------|---------------------|---------------------|

    Nothing   A Little   A Moderate Amount   Quite A Bit   A Great Deal

3. How much emotion did you feel during this learning experience?

    |---------------------|---------------------|---------------------|---------------------|---------------------|

    Nothing   A Little   A Moderate Amount   Quite A Bit   A Great Deal

4. How much general anxiety or fear did you feel during this learning experience?

    |---------------------|---------------------|---------------------|---------------------|---------------------|

    Nothing   A Little   A Moderate Amount   Quite A Bit   A Great Deal

5. How much general sadness or depression did you feel during this learning experience?

    |---------------------|---------------------|---------------------|---------------------|---------------------|

    Nothing   A Little   A Moderate Amount   Quite A Bit   A Great Deal

6. How much feelings of sorrow about your offense behavior did you feel during this learning experience?

    |---------------------|---------------------|---------------------|---------------------|---------------------|

    Nothing   A Little   A Moderate Amount   Quite A Bit   A Great Deal

7. How much concern and worry about how your survivor(s) will turn out did you feel during this learning experience?

    |---------------------|---------------------|---------------------|---------------------|---------------------|

    Nothing   A Little   A Moderate Amount   Quite A Bit   A Great Deal

8. How much regret (wishing you could take it back) did you feel during this learning experience?

    |---------------------|---------------------|---------------------|---------------------|---------------------|

    Nothing   A Little   A Moderate Amount   Quite A Bit   A Great Deal

9. How much self-disgust about your offense behavior did you feel during this learning experience?

    |---------------------|---------------------|---------------------|---------------------|---------------------|

    Nothing   A Little   A Moderate Amount   Quite A Bit   A Great Deal

10. How much feelings of guilt about your offense behavior did you feel during this learning experience?

    |---------------------|---------------------|---------------------|---------------------|---------------------|

    Nothing   A Little   A Moderate Amount   Quite A Bit   A Great Deal

11. How much feelings of anger at yourself for your behavior did you experience during this learning experience?

    |---------------------|---------------------|---------------------|---------------------|---------------------|

    Nothing   A Little   A Moderate Amount   Quite A Bit   A Great Deal

12. How much fear of facing what you did and the people you offended did you feel during this learning experience?

|---------------------|---------------------|---------------------|---------------------|
Nothing   A Little   A Moderate Amount   Quite A Bit   A Great Deal

13. How much fear about someone getting even with you for your offenses did you feel during this learning experience?

|---------------------|---------------------|---------------------|---------------------|
Nothing   A Little   A Moderate Amount   Quite A Bit   A Great Deal

14. How much fear of feeling powerless, helpless, or not in control did you feel during this learning experience?

|---------------------|---------------------|---------------------|---------------------|
Nothing   A Little   A Moderate Amount   Quite A Bit   A Great Deal

15. How much did this learning experience get you in touch with how selfish and inconsiderate of others you were?

|---------------------|---------------------|---------------------|---------------------|
Nothing   A Little   A Moderate Amount   Quite A Bit   A Great Deal

16. How much did this learning experience get you in touch with how selfish and inconsiderate of others you were?

|---------------------|---------------------|---------------------|---------------------|
Nothing   A Little   A Moderate Amount   Quite A Bit   A Great Deal

17. How much did this learning experience get you in touch with the amount of damage you did to others?

|---------------------|---------------------|---------------------|---------------------|
Nothing   A Little   A Moderate Amount   Quite A Bit   A Great Deal

18. How much more did this learning experience get you thinking about others' thoughts and feelings?

|---------------------|---------------------|---------------------|---------------------|
Nothing   A Little   A Moderate Amount   Quite A Bit   A Great Deal

19. How much did this learning experience get you in touch with the fact that no matter what you thought or felt, you had no right to offend against another person?

|---------------------|---------------------|---------------------|---------------------|
Nothing   A Little   A Moderate Amount   Quite A Bit   A Great Deal

20. How much did this learning experience get you in touch with the fact that you were making excuses for your behavior?

|---------------------|---------------------|---------------------|---------------------|
Nothing   A Little   A Moderate Amount   Quite A Bit   A Great Deal

21. How much did this learning experience get you in touch with the fact that nothing the survivor did caused the offense; it was completely your fault and responsibility?

|---------------------|---------------------|---------------------|---------------------|
Nothing   A Little   A Moderate Amount   Quite A Bit   A Great Deal

22. How beneficial was this learning experience to you in terms of motivating you to avoid re-offense?

|---------------------|---------------------|---------------------|---------------------|
Nothing   A Little   A Moderate Amount   Quite A Bit   A Great Deal

23. Please comment on what affected you the most about this learning experience.

_____

_____

Appendix B-2
BEHAVIOR CONTRACT FOR SURVIVOR IMPACT SESSION

I agree to conduct myself in a responsible and appropriate manner before, during, and after I attend the Survivor Impact Session that has been scheduled for me. I will do this by cooperating with the following guidelines:

Before:

I will not attempt to speak with the survivors before the session.

I will enter the group room before the survivors and make sure that I am seated when they arrive.

If I recognize any of the survivors from school or the community, I will inform my therapist at once so that the issue of excusing me from the group can be discussed.

During:

I will follow all Youth Sex Offender group rules. I will follow all of my survivor safety standards.

I will speak to the survivors only when they ask me a question or when asked to do so by one of the group therapists.

If I have the occasion to speak with the survivors, I will maintain language and behavior that is not sexual, aggressive or dishonest.

After:

I will not attempt to hug or speak with the survivors privately after the session. I understand that I may request to shake the survivor's hands and thank them in the presence of their therapist.

If I recognize any of the survivors while at school or out in the community, I will not approach them or speak with them and will report this to my therapist at once.

If one of the survivors from the impact session recognizes me at school or in the community and speaks to me, I will politely tell them that I am not allowed to speak to them according to my program rules. I will report this to my therapist at once.

I understand and agree to conduct my behavior in the manner described above.

Signature: _____   Date: _____

Witness: _____   Date: _____

Appendix B-3
THOUGHTS AND FEELINGS QUESTIONNAIRE

Name: _____   Date: _____

Birthdate: _____   Sex: _____

How many months have you been in therapy? _____

What type of therapy are you in (Group/Individual/Family) and how often do you attend? _____

Please use the scales below to mark any changes in your feelings or thoughts which you have had *since the time* you spoke with the Youth Sex Offenders.

1. Feeling guilty about or blaming self.

    |--------------------|--------------------|--------------------|--------------------|
    Much more   A little more   About the same   A little less   Much less

2. Feeling afraid or anxious.

    |--------------------|--------------------|--------------------|--------------------|
    Much more   A little more   About the same   A little less   Much less

3. Feeling sad and depressed.

    |--------------------|--------------------|--------------------|--------------------|
    Much more   A little more   About the same   A little less   Much less

4. Thinking "I'm damaged" and will never be the same.

    |--------------------|--------------------|--------------------|--------------------|
    Much more   A little more   About the same   A little less   Much less

5. Feeling inadequate or not as good as others.

    |--------------------|--------------------|--------------------|--------------------|
    Much more   A little more   About the same   A little less   Much less

6. Feeling angry or hostile.

    |-------------------- --|--------------------|--------------------|--------------------|
    Much more   A little more   About the same   A little less   Much less

7. Thinking you can't trust people.

    |--------------------|--------------------|--------------------|--------------------|
    Much more   A little more   About the same   A little less   Much less

8. Feeling helpless or not in control of what happens to me.

    |--------------------|--------------------|--------------------|--------------------|
    Much more   A little more   About the same   A little less   Much less

9. Has anything happened to you since the time that you spoke with the Youth Sex Offenders that could have affected your feelings one way or the other?

    _____

10. Please describe how coming face-to-face and speaking with or confronting the sex offenders has helped or hurt you.

    _____

11. Would you recommend that other survivors be given the opportunity to confront offenders or speak to them face-to-face? Why?

    _____

Appendix C-1
PARENT/GUARDIAN QUESTIONNAIRE
(after apology letter and session)

Note: This questionnaire should be completed in the presence of a mental health professional who can discuss any feelings or answer any questions that you might have about it. Your answers are very important to us and we will use them to decide whether to continue to use apology letters or sessions in our therapy.

Name: _____   Date: _____

1. How long ago did you receive   _____
   the apology letter?

2. Are you involved in therapy? ___Yes; ___No If yes, how long? _____
   What type of therapy? (_individual; _family; _group)

3. Is or was the SURVIVOR in therapy? ___Yes; ___No; ___Don't Know
   a. How long have they been going to therapy sessions?_____
   b. In your opinion or from what you know, how much have they been able to talk about their abuse in therapy sessions?

   |------------------------|------------------------|------------------------|------------------------|
   None   A little   Moderately   Quite a bit   Completely

   c. In your opinion or from what you know, how well are they dealing with their feelings about being abused?

   |------------------------|------------------------|------------------------|------------------------|
   Not at all   A little   Moderately   Quite a bit   Completely

   d. Would it be helpful if you knew more about how well they were adjusting? ___ Yes; ___ No; ___ I am well informed

4. Is or was the OFFENDER in therapy? ___Yes; ___No; ___Don't Know
   a. How long have they been going to therapy sessions?_____
   b. In your opinion or from what you know, how much have they been willing to discuss about their offense behavior in therapy sessions?

   |------------------------|------------------------|------------------------|------------------------|
   None   A little   Moderately   Quite a bit   Completely

   c. In your opinion or from what you know, how well are they cooperating with therapy guidelines and
      controlling their behavior?

   |------------------------|------------------------|------------------------|------------------------|
   Not at all   A little   Moderately   Quite a bit   Completely

   d. Would it be helpful if you knew more about how much they were cooperating with therapy? ___ Yes; ___ No; ___ I am well informed

5. Please mark your opinion below on how receiving the apology SESSION has helped or hurt you.

	Much more	A little more	About the same	A little less	Much less
Accept what happened	|-----------|-----------|-----------|-----------|				
Be able to discuss the abuse	|-----------|-----------|-----------|-----------|				
Feeling guilty/blaming self	|-----------|-----------|-----------|-----------|				
Feeling worried or anxious	|-----------|-----------|-----------|-----------|				
Feeling sad and depressed	|-----------|-----------|-----------|-----------|				
Feeling angry or hostile	|-----------|-----------|-----------|-----------|				

6. Please list any other ways that receiving the apology SESSION has helped or hurt you.
   _____

7. Based on your experience with this apology session, would you recommend that other parents/guardians be given the opportunity to receive offender apology SESSIONS? ___Yes; ___No

Parent/Guardian Questionnaire, Page 2

8. Please mark your opinion below on how receiving the apology LETTER has helped or hurt you.

	Much More	A little more	About the same	A little less	Much less
Accept what happened		------------	------------	------------	------------	
Be able to discuss the abuse		------------	------------	------------	------------	
Honesty about your feelings		------------	------------	------------	------------	
Feeling guilty/blaming self		------------	------------	------------	------------	
Feeling worried or anxious		------------	------------	------------	------------	
Feeling sad and depressed		------------	------------	------------	------------	
Feeling angry or hostile		------------	------------	------------	------------	

9. Please list any other ways that receiving the apology LETTER has helped or hurt you.

_____

10. Based on your experience with this apology letter, would you recommend that other parents/guardians be given the opportunity to receive offender apology LETI'ERS? ___Yes; ___No

Appendix C-2
CLIENT QUESTIONNAIRE
(apology session)

Instructions: Please complete this questionnaire after discussing the apology session with your therapist or advocate.

Name: _____   Date:_____

1. How many therapy sessions have you had since you received the apology session? _____ (or if you are not in therapy), how long ago did you receive the apology session? _____

2. Please use the graphs below to mark your opinion on how receiving the apology session has helped or hurt you.

	Much more	A little more	About the same	A little less	Much less
Accept what happened	|------------|------------|------------|------------|
Be open to giving details	|------------|------------|------------|------------|
Honesty about your feelings	|------------|------------|------------|------------|
Feeling guilty/blaming self	|------------|------------|------------|------------|
Feeling afraid or anxious	|------------|------------|------------|------------|
Feeling sad and depressed	|------------|------------|------------|------------|
Feeling angry or hostile	|------------|------------|------------|------------|

3. Please list any other ways that receiving the apology session has helped or hurt you.

_____
_____
_____
_____

4. Based on your experience with this apology session, would you recommend that other survivors be given the opportunity to receive offender apology sessions? Why?

_____
_____
_____
_____

THERAPIST OR VICTIM ADVOCATE QUESTIONNAIRE
(apology session)

Instructions: Please complete this questionnaire after discussing the apology session with...

Name: _____   Date:_____

Please mark your relationship to the client: ___therapist; ___victim advocate;

___other (Please list _____)

1. Please use the graphs below to mark your opinion on how receiving the apology session has helped or hurt your client's treatment or emotional well-being.

	Much more	A little more	About the same	A little less	Much less
Denial of happened	I------------I------------I------------I------------I				
Openness to giving details	I------------I------------I------------I------------I				
Honesty about feelings	I------------I------------I------------I------------I				
Guilt or self-blame	I------------I------------I------------I------------I				
Fear and anxiety	I------------I------------I------------I------------I				
Sadness/Depression	I------------I------------I------------I------------I				
Anger/Hostility	I------------I------------I------------I------------I				

2. Please list any other aspects of your treatment or your client's well-being that has been helped or hurt by receiving the apology session.

   _____
   _____
   _____
   _____

3. Based on your experience with this apology session, would you recommend that other professionals be given the opportunity to use offender apology sessions to help survivors? Why?

   _____
   _____
   _____
   _____

Appendix C-3
THINGS I WANT TO KNOW

One problem that often comes up in the treatment of sexual abuse survivors is that the survivors are left feeling hurt as well as confused because they are unable to understand the offender's behavior. The directors of both the survivor and offender treatment programs in Stark County have been discussing a plan of how to help the survivors in treatment get the information that they need from the offenders in order to decrease their confused feelings. They have decided to conduct an Offender Information Group and make a videotape where the offenders answer questions that you would like to ask.

Please fill out the questionnaire on what you would like to know about your offender. Fill out one of these forms for each person that committed a sexual offense against you. If you decide to attend the Offender Information Group after discussing this issue with your therapist, you may ask any of the questions that you have listed below.

Today's Date: _____

Your First name: _____   Your age: _____   Your sex: _____

Offenders First name: _____   Offenders age: _____ Offenders sex: _____

If you could, what would you like to ask the offender about their behavior towards you (or survivors in general)?

_____

_____

_____

What would you like to know about the offender as a person?

_____

_____

_____

Appendix D
SURVIVORS' PSYCHOLOGICAL TEST SCORES BEFORE AND AFTER THE SURVIVOR IMPACT GROUP

Test Administered	Survivor	Age	Score Before		Score After[21]	
Beck Depression Inventory	#1	18	11		9	
	#2	17	0		0	
	#3	18	0		1	
	#4	11	6		Didn't Attend	
	#5	13	13		Didn't Attend	
State-Trait Anxiety Inventory			State	Trait	State	Trait
	#1		43	49	57	44
	#2		44	41	38	39
	#3		41	33	40	35
	#4		52	47	Didn't Attend	
	#5		50	54	Didn't Attend	
Rotter Locus of Control Scale	#1		16		15	
	#2		10		8	
	#3		9		8	
	#4		13		Didn't Attend	
	#5		8		Didn't Attend	

Age and Psychological Test Score Differences Between Survivor Volunteers Who Attended Versus Did Not Attend the Survivor Impact Group

	Average Ages	Average Test Scores			
		Depression	Anxiety		Locus of Control
			State	Trait	
Attended (#1,2,3)	17.7	3.7	42.7	41.0	11.7
Didn't Attend (#4,5)	12.0	9.5	51.0	50.5	10.5

On all three test measures administered, lower scores indicate less intense symptoms. Although adolescent norms for the Beck Depression Inventory are not currently established, scores ranging from O to 9 are generally considered within the normal range. On the State-Trait Anxiety Inventory, T-Scores are provided. T- Scores are set up such that the average person's score is-50 and the majority (66%) will score between 40 and 60 which is considered within normal limits. Locus of Control Scale scores for female, Ohio, 12th-grade students ranging from 4 to 11 can be considered within the normal range.

21. Post-test taken one week after the Survivor Impact Group session.

Appendix E
OFFENDER RESPONSES TO THE SURVIVOR IMPACT GROUP

The offender responses listed below were in answer to the question "What affected you most" about the Survivor Impact Group.[22]

"The part that affected me the most was that they said that what was done to them will always be there and it will never go away." (Written by a 16-year-old, white male who molested his stepsister.)

"That point that [Jan] made was all sex abuse is just a few minutes of pleasure to destroy a person's whole life." (Written by a 16-year-old, white male who violently molested his stepbrother.)

"Everything, it was very upsetting hearing what they went through and are still going through and will go through because of people like me." (Written by a 15-year-old, white male who molested his niece.)

"That I had no right to do what I did." (Written by a 17-year-old, white male who molested a neighbor boy.)

"When [Jan] and [Lynn] asked how could someone do this and when they were talking about the way they felt." (Written by Ron.)

"Finding out exactly how the survivor really feels being victimized and it never leaves them day or night." (Written by a 17-year-old, white male who molested multiple male victims.)

"The fact that their families won't have anything to do with them, but still talk to and allow the person who victimized them to come around." (Written by a 15-year-old, white male who molested multiple child victims of both genders.)

"I couldn't look at the survivors. I pictured my own victims in their place." (Written by a 17-year-old, white male who molested multiple child victims of both genders and one incapacitated adult.)

"Why did I ever do this to another person? I wish I was dead." (Written by a 17-year-old, white male exhibitionist.)

"It all affected me in a way that words cannot express only feelings can. I think this will help me to speak more freely." (Written by a 15-year-old, white male who molested a neighbor girl.)

"The people who were survivors and how they helped me understand more about what I did to [Cheryl]. I think thank you letters should be written to thank them." (Written by a 19-year-old, white male who molested his foster sister.)

---

22. **Note:** Not all offenders commented; the one inappropriate response ("I'd like to date the three panelists") was not communicated to the survivors.

Appendix F
SURVIVOR AND OFFENDER PSYCHOLOGICAL TEST SCORES BEFORE AND AFTER THE OFFENDER INFORMATION GROUP[23]

Test Administered	Participant and Age	Test Score Before Group			Test Score After Group		
State-Trait Anxiety Inventory		State	Trait		State	Trait	
	VI 19	44	43		40	44	
	V2 16	40	40		41	39	
	V3 15	49	59		55	65	
	V4 15	42	48		43	45	
	V5 14	60	73		68	71	
Ron →	O1 18	69	57		41	44	
	O2 19	72	64		38	58	
	O3 18	69	52		81	51	
State-Trait Anger Inventory		State	Trait	(T&R)	State	Trait	(T&R)
	VI 19	53	41	46 40	55	41	49 35
	V2 16	54	57	55 63	46	47	46 57
	V3 15	57	58	62 60	54	57	62 60
	V4 15	46	48	57 40	46	47	52 44
	V5 14	61	69	80 57	65	69	80 57
Ron →	O1 18	50	47	53 46	46	49	53 46
	O2 19	56	49	53 50	55	49	50 52
	O3 18	46	37	42 55	65	37	47 62

On both test measures administered, lower scores indicate less intense symptoms. Both test measures administered before and after the offender information session provided T-Scores (average score is 50 and 66% of those tested, score between 40 and 60 which is within normal limits).

The results of the offender testing before and after the offender information session revealed the following. Both offender State Anxiety and Trait Anxiety decreased (an average of 6.7 and 6.7 points per offender respectively). Offender State Anger and Angry Reaction increased (an average of 4.7 and 3.0 points respectively), due to one offender who experienced a strong anger reaction towards himself and other offenders for their behavior. Trait Anger and Angry Temperament stayed about the same (an average increase of .7 points per offender for both measures).

In summary, of the 18 anger and anxiety test measures taken on the offenders who conducted the offender information session, 14 (78%) of the posttest scores were about the same (within 2 points) or lower than the pretest scores.

---

23. Pre- and posttest administered just before and after session. (T & R) = Angry Temperament & Angry Reaction subscales of State-Trait Anger Expression Inventory.

Social Solutions Press Books

Other books related to social responsibility in psychotherapy by Social Solutions Press, available at socialsolutionspress.org or Amazon.com Include...

The Clinician's Guide to Social Responsibility Therapy

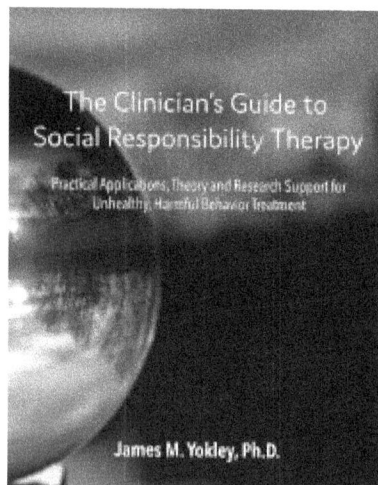

Social Responsibility Therapy (SRT) was designed to help develop social responsibility in clients with multiple forms of unhealthy, harmful behavior from multiple cultural backgrounds. The Clinicians Guide to SRT was written to benefit clinicians in treatment programs or independent practice with clients who exhibit one or more forms of unhealthy, harmful behavior. This guide provides in depth clinician-focused treatment coverage of the four SRT "Healthy Behavior Success Skills" used to help clients pull themselves towards positive change (internal control); the structure needed to help push clients towards positive change (external control) and; the "Healthy Relationship Success Skills" needed to develop a positive recovery network (social learning). The Clinicians Guide to SRT integrates theory and research support into practical clinical applications of SRT skills and concepts illustrated with case examples.

Practical Applications, Theory and Research Support for Unhealthy, Harmful Behavior Treatment, North Myrtle Beach, SC: Social Solutions Press. 2016, 301 pages. ISBN: 978-0-9832449-4-3.

Social Responsibility Therapy for Adolescents & Young Adults

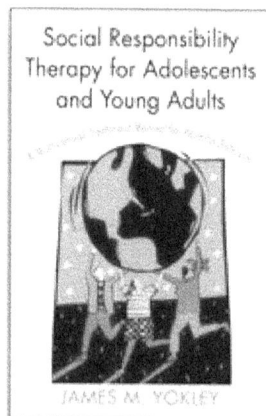

This crucial treatment manual that can be used by mental health professionals whose caseload includes a multicultural population of adolescents and young adults who exhibit multiple forms of harmful behavior. This unique therapy enhances relapse prevention in harmful behavior treatment by addressing the target behavior problem, negative social influence problem, and dose-response problem, along with acknowledging that harmful behavior is multicultural and addressing the key criticisms of multicultural therapy through a theory-driven treatment approach that utilizes methods and procedures from existing evidence-based treatments with known multicultural applications.

A Multicultural Treatment Manual for Harmful Behavior, New York, NY, US: Routledge/Taylor & Francis Group. 2008, 357 pages. ISBN: 978-0-7890-3121-1.

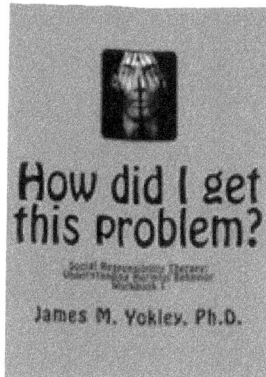

How did I get this problem?

This Social Responsibility Therapy workbook was designed to help individuals who are struggling with unhealthy, harmful behaviors such as problem eating, drinking, drugs, physical or sexual aggression, answer the question, "How did I get this problem?"

Social Responsibility Therapy: Understanding Harmful Behavior Workbook 1. Social Solutions Press.
2010, 123 pages. ISBN: 978-0-9832449-0-5.

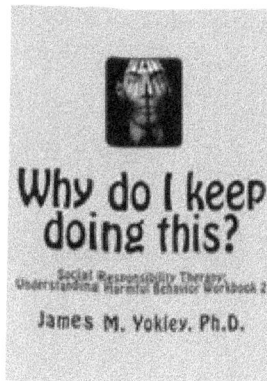

Why do I keep doing this?

This Social Responsibility Therapy workbook was designed to help individuals who are struggling with unhealthy, harmful behaviors such as problem eating, drinking, drugs, physical or sexual aggression, answer the question, "Why do I keep doing this?"

Social Responsibility Therapy: Understanding Harmful Behavior Workbook 2. Social Solutions Press.
2011, 143 pages. ISBN: 978-0-9832449-1-2.

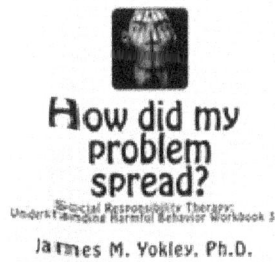

How did my problem spread?

This workbook describes ten Harmful Behavior Anatomy components that contribute to the growth and spread of unhealthy, harmful behavior. Mental health professionals and clients can work together to develop brief skills-based treatment plans by focusing on the specific components that contribute most to the individuals unhealthy harmful behavior.

Social Responsibility Therapy: Understanding Harmful Behavior Workbook 3: Social Solutions Press.
2012, 237 pages. ISBN: 978-0-9832449-2-9.

www.ingramcontent.com/pod-product-compliance
Lightning Source LLC
Chambersburg PA
CBHW080052280326
41934CB00014B/3287